the 4C Heart

CURLS, KINKS, AND KNOTS OF MY DRY, THIRSTY, SINGLE SOUL

the 4C Heart

CURLS, KINKS, AND KNOTS OF MY DRY, THIRSTY, SINGLE SOUL

MY JOURNAL JOURNEY
INTO WOMANHOOD

Anna E. Styron

Copyright © 2022 by Anna E. Styron

All rights reserved. This book or parts of it may not be reproduced in any form without permission in writing from the publisher, except that a reviewer may quote brief passages in a review.

Anna E. Styron
Garner, US
4cheartseries@gmail.com

ISBN: 978-1-7367370-4-0 (Paperback)
ISBN: 978-1-7367370-3-3 (eBook)

Library of Congress Control Number: 2022912198

Printed in the United States of America
First Edition, 2022

Cover and interior book design by Jonathan Sainsbury
Illustrations by Valentina Migliore
Copy-Edited by Abbey McLaughlin

Note to the Readers	xi
Introduction	xiii
Love Hurts: A sacrifice made only for the humble and the strong-willed	1
Broken Pieces	13
Journal Journey Entries	27
Closing Though and Prayer	63
About the Author	69

Dedication

Jayden and Janiah, you two have always been the reasons I get up every morning and push myself so hard. Your gift of life inspired me and motivated me to do better and to become a better woman, mother, and Christ follower. Thank you. I love you both so much!

To my family and friends, thank you for your prayers throughout my journey. They have meant so much to me. God bless you.

To the ministries who have helped me grow throughout the seasons of my life, especially EX Ministries, thank you.

It is not a bad thing to be thirsty.

"Blessed are those who hunger and thirst
for righteousness, for they shall be filled."
Matthew 5:6 (NKJV)

Note to the Readers

"What is a *4C Heart?* It is basically a condition of a heart that takes the characteristics of 4C hair. Black hair, like the heart, can be very complex. Our hair has various curl patterns which range from type 2A (loose waves) to type 4C (tight coils). Essentially, most Black women have curly (3) or kinky (4) hair. The A, B, and C refer to the diameter of the curl. 4C hair is densely packed, experiences the most shrinkage, and the strands are so tightly coiled that they are incredibly delicate. In general, 4C hair needs a lot of moisture and hydration in order to thrive. The unique characteristic of tightness, softness, proneness to breakage, and potential dryness are the same characteristics I use to describe my own heart. Just as caring for 4C curls requires a bit of effort and patience. It is the same way we must care for the matters of the heart. Just as 4C hair requires finding curl care products with the right ingredients, so is obtaining healthy strategies and skills for healing of the heart. Just as there are certain ingredients you should steer clear of with 4C hair that may strip the hair of its natural oils and make it prone to damage, we must protect and guard our hearts from things that are not life giving. Just as a day and night routine is valuable to the care of the 4C hair, so is the same for cultivating and maintaining a healthy condition of the heart. 4C hair requires a lot of tender loving care (TLC), but the benefits of embracing this texture is so worth it. And so are the benefits for the healing of your heart, mind, body, and soul.

Women of God, it is time for us to heal. Be gracious with yourself and allow your soul time to develop tastebuds for health. I pray that this series ministers to your heart, mind, body, and soul as I share my journey through life. May you be blessed and then be a blessing to someone else's life in return. Jesus loves you, and so do I. Amen.

Introduction

> "He has put a new song in my mouth—
> Praise to our God; Many will see it and fear.
> And will trust in the LORD."—Psalm 40:3 (NKJV)

As women, we are given the gift to be emotional (yes, it is a gift, not a fault, not a weakness). We are also given the gift to be nurturing and to be sensitive to the supernatural. These are the reasons why Satan came to the woman in the Garden of Eden. He knew there was something about the woman and what she carries. Women carry a womb, which carries the bloodlines of the next generation. Heaven has a desired generational narrative, but so does hell. Satan knew in that moment that if he could plant a seed of identity confusion, then he could play on Eve's emotions and feed her the biggest, most detrimental lie: that humans are not enough, even though God told us we were perfect when He created us!

This is a lie of insecurity that plagues the minds of women today. We do not amount to enough. We are not pretty enough, not interesting enough, not creative enough, not skilled enough, not competitive enough, not strong enough, not brave enough, not thin enough, not thick enough, not dark enough, not light enough, not black/white/Asian/Hispanic/Indian enough, not smart enough, not feminine enough, not health conscientious enough, not wealthy enough, not accomplished enough, not independent enough, not married or having kids soon enough, not busy enough, not attentive enough, not liberal enough, not conservative enough, not spiritual enough, not "woke" enough, not woman enough . . . and the lies go on.

This is the lie that weighed me down for so long. It played on repeat throughout years: the song of failure and defeat, the song of confusion, the song of emptiness, the song of anxiety and depression, the song of doubt, and the song of regret.

Well, know this, woman of God: the lie that is the most repetitious, most consistent, and most dominant is where you are the most dangerous! So, thank God for that insight! He gave me a new song! And He is giving you a new song! You and I have a standard, and we must understand the value of what we carry. God reminded me that I am His creation. I am enough in Him. It is okay to embrace my womanhood without shame. No need to be anyone or anything else but you, a woman.

Lift your head up high. Let your tears flow. Embrace your journey into womanhood.

> "And who knows but that you have come to your royal position for such a time as this?"
> —Esther 4:14 (NIV)

Love Hurts

A Sacrifice Made Only for the Humble and the Strong-Willed

❧ *A Rose from the Grave*

Do you ever wish you could turn back the hands of time? Just back a couple of days, months, or years even? If you only knew then what you know now. That's what I've always heard mature people say. So far, I've found it to be true, too. I wondered often how my life ended up this way? I was the good girl. I had the looks, the smarts, the personality, so why am I stuck back in my parent's house with two kids, no job, and a tear-soaked pillow full of regrets? I should never have stopped to look his way. If only my roommate and I had gone for groceries the day before, the day after, the day never! I would have never seen him, met him, or even wanted to get to know him. I would have never told my girl to "show that chick he's with how it's really done on the court." That basketball game would have never been played, and I would have never fallen in love (or what I thought was love at the time). If only this, if only that.

I wonder if these thoughts run through your mind at night too, with tears of regret, shame, and anger just pouring down. Why didn't we ever see this coming?

Our lives tell a story. Each life on this earth is a single chapter in the great Book of Life. All our deeds recorded, every single white lie, every single muttered word, and every single hidden secret. Is your book a love story? A thriller? I would like to think of my life as a mystery. I just do not know what is going to happen next. I thought I had it all planned out, and then the next thing you know, something unexplained and unexpected popped up. Will it ever make sense? Seeing the big picture is so hard for me. I feel like I am digging and digging, and just when I think I see the light and can feel the sunshine warm my frigid hands, it pours down rain, and I am back where I started.

I can feel the vibrations of the feet overhead of those so-called friends stomping above me, and hear the laughter of the so-called husband asking me, "Where is your God now? How come He cannot just pull you out of there and bring you back on top like the rest of us?" Rage just burns up within me, but then I stop.

Where are you, God? Why am I drowning in all these troubles? Why am I the one down here suffering all alone? You said You would never leave me nor forsake me. I am supposed to be the Christian who serves an Almighty God. So why is my unsaved husband and all of his buddies and their friends out there getting their degrees, cars, and homes, and I am stuck down here with the kids and nothing to show for my time? Why don't you talk to me?

Rage and anger wrap their warm arms around me, but I know I cannot sit in this pity party for long. I have to throw them off and get on my knees and pray. The only way is to start digging out of this hole all over again. I know the answers to my questions. I know why I am here. I know how I got here. I know it is not God's doing; it is my own. So, the real question is can I live with it and move on? If God is patient with us in our rebellion, why can't we be patient with Him in our healing?

When I was a little girl, I had set some goals for myself for things I wanted to do, wanted to be, and wanted to have. I wanted to travel the world, be a nurse, have my nose pierced and get a tattoo, and I wanted to get married and stay home to raise my kids. That was it! Very simple. When I was a young lady, I had set some goals for myself of things I *never* wanted to do, never wanted to be, and never wanted to have. I told myself that I would never join the military, never be divorced, and never get an abortion. Isn't it crazy how those two got so mixed up? What happened? What went wrong? I will tell you.

I told God that He was not for me. I put Him on the shelf and told Him when my parents come to visit or when Sunday rolls around, do not worry, I will dust You off and You will be as good as if I had used You every day of my life. Who was I fooling telling everyone that I was a Christian and out partying and drinking every weekend? Just myself! Of course it was fun. What is done in secret can be very fun! Who wouldn't enjoy wild, crazy sex every night from their man outside of marriage? We said we loved each other, so that counts right? Who wouldn't love club hopping every weekend to grab the attention and intentions of every man in the building? Who wouldn't like to drink away their sorrows and numb their pain for a while? I know I did. That was my life. I loved the attention. Too bad it all comes with a price. Unfortunately, I could not afford it.

So now, I am digging. Digging my grave to die because my debt is too high, and I cannot afford it.

My boyfriend and I were expecting an unplanned baby, and I could not afford to shame myself in that way. I was not ready. My parents would be so disappointed. I just started my military career. The only way out was an abortion. *Keep digging.*

My boyfriend and I broke up, and I found out he was messing with another woman, so I befriended another man and slept with him. He didn't know, and I would never tell him. That would fix that situation. *Keep digging.*

My life was so confusing that I asked my friends to take me out for a good time. I ended up making out with a white boy who wanted to take me home and almost does. Am I turning into a slut? Why did I almost go there? *Keep digging.*

I was trying so hard to turn my life around, but my boyfriend (yeah, I stupidly took him back) kept telling me to let him help me.

Just trust him. Just keep him around and my life will turn around. *Keep digging.*

I became pregnant again, but this time I was keeping the baby. Now, what do I do? Pastors, family, and friends tried to tell me not to rush into marriage and to put the baby up for adoption. We were not ready. We have not even gone to counseling. My boyfriend promised me the world. We kissed before the magistrate in "holy" matrimony. *Keep digging.*

I found my husband having affairs with other women online, numerous phone numbers and names in his phone. I almost threw him out, but he finally promised to go to counseling. I found out I was pregnant again, and after a while, counseling is put on hold. *Still digging.*

My husband reverted to his old ways, and picked up drinking, smoking, and partying all night, leaving me home alone in pain with contractions from early labor. *I lay down in my grave. My pulse steadily drops.*

After my daughter was born, things change. I start to change. My feelings toward my husband start to change. The pressures of work and rearing the kids by myself were so immense that I started to wear down. What happened to the promises made by my husband? I realized I chose and accepted the wrong man in my life. *My heart stops.*

The dirt drops heavily onto my body and slowly begins to cover my face. With my last breath, I pray to God. I ask for forgiveness. I ask for another chance. I realize that I do need Him in my life. He is not a trophy God to pull off the shelf when I need that kind of recognition. He is an all-time God that requires full-time service from me. I want to stop digging. I do not want to die in my sins.

For so long, I had been suicidal. For so long, I had wanted to just die and end it all. But I knew better. I knew that I was not ready to meet my Maker. Not like this. I did not want to spend eternity in any more anguish than I already was in. *Save me, Lord! Save me!*

Some say that when they receive Christ into their heart, they burst into tears, or laugh hysterically, or jumped up and down. Some say they felt a warm sensation flow through them or shook uncontrollably. My experience was all the above! I felt chains just drop off my hands and feet. My body just shook out of control. Tears flowed from my eyes. I laughed for the first time in my life from pure joy.

My time was not up yet. It was not time for me to go. I messed up big time, but I have a purpose to fulfill still. Devil, you have messed up now. You thought you had me, didn't you? Yeah, you had me fooled! Dressed as the man who would give me the world, but your cover is blown! I am no longer under your control! You messed with the wrong woman! Yeah, I have a lot of digging to do to get out of this grave, but you will not stop me. I rebuke you in the name of Jesus. You no longer have any control or power over me. I serve a greater Lord, a mighty God, and He will raise me up! It is going to be a while before I am on top, but when I get there, you better beware! This woman of God is on fire!

I do not know where my life is headed. I do not know what is going to happen. But I do know I have Jesus. I do know there will never be anyone to take His place. It is going to be hard raising two kids on my own. I know it is not God's order for there to be only one parent in the home. But I am going to have to trust God in this situation. I will not try to fix it on my own again. I will not give Satan the satisfaction. Grave, you have no victory! And death, you have no sting!

I pray that my life will be an inspiration to someone else. A warning to another. You may think you know more and want to live your own life. I know because I said the same thing. I thought my life was so boring and my parents were too strict. I wanted to live! I envied those people who gave their testimony of what they went through before they got saved. I looked at my life and thought, *I can't give a testimony.* My life is too boring to testify about. Why can't I go through something dramatic like that? Oh, so foolish!

Have you ever heard that you have the ability to speak into existence what you want to happen in your life? Well, it is true. I spoke every single hurt and pain I went through into my life. If only I had known how powerful my words were. Like a two-edged sword, you can hurt someone with your tongue, and you can do some damage to your own life. How I wish I could take those prophecies back. But I cannot. The damage is done, and the scars are still healing. Life is about God. Not about us.

From dust, we came, and dust we will return. The focus of our lives belongs to God. If your life seems boring, you are probably not living for God the way you should! There is not a dull moment when He is truly in your life. There is so much to do, so much to learn!

And not enough days, hours, minutes, or seconds to do it all. Even if you are not outgoing, or if you are scared to death to talk to people about God, there are other ways. Use your strengths to minister: song, dance, writing, sports, driving, cooking/baking, drumming, fitness, drawing, painting, gaming, hosting, drama, sewing, crocheting, gardening, makeup, hair, modeling—anything can be used for God's glory. Live your life! But most importantly, live it for God!

❀ *Raped Rose*

Jesus loved us so much that He was willing to die for us. That love nailed Him to a painful, agonizing death on a cross. That love pierced a sword through His side. That love crowned His head with thorns. That love cost Him his last breath. His love was a sacrifice of His own life. Who did God love so much that He was willing to die? You and me, the least deserving creatures on this earth. The ones who turned our backs on him when life was going good. The ones who laughed at Him when He did not dress, talk, or walk as we did. The ones who spit in His face and ridiculed Him when He spoke truth into our lives. For it says in His Word that whatever we did to the least of those, we did to Him (Matthew 25:40-45).

He loved us enough to die. It hurt, but He was humble enough to continue the walk of shame and strong enough to stay on that cross because of His love for us. He knew that if He did not do it, did not complete this task, we would die not only in the physical but in the spiritual. To live eternally in heaven would be just a dream. But it is not. It is a true reality. We have that choice now because of this. So, is this why true love hurts? It is true that what does not kill you makes you stronger? Well, I believe true love hurts. If it did not, our world would not be in the mess it was in today. True love hurts our pride, hurts our lusts, hurts our selfishness, and hurts our flesh.

So, you thought that was the end? Another happy ending? I finally found love, met my prince, rode off into the clouds, and lived happily ever after? All my troubles and worries over, right? Wrong. It was far from that.

Never had I imagined what kind of road I would walk down next—a repeat of the same song, yet a different tune. So, I sit here and wonder, *how and why?* After all that I went through before, why didn't I, couldn't I, have seen these miseries coming? Shovel in hand once more, I began to dig another grave.

LUST OF THE EYE

He was a good and upright man. He was a pastor of a small congregation. He said all the right things at the right times. He understood my frustrations, my worries, my doubts, and my fears. I had even told him something about me that was locked up in the dark, hidden. Something that no one else knew about me. I could trust him, and he seemed to understand. In fact, he told me that it was natural and a blessing. I had never heard that before.

Something inside me felt conflicted, but I pushed it aside. He was a pastor. A man that walked with the Lord God Almighty himself. If this man says it, I believe it. What was I thinking? I wasn't. The next thing I know, I was talking to the other woman in his life. His fiancé. She said she had heard so much about me. She told me that she has been with other women before, but when she met the pastor, she wanted to be with him only. But, since he loved me too, she was willing to share. She was informed about my curiosity with another woman, and she would love to show me. She enticed me with her words. She thrilled me with her guilty pleasures. She made me feel good just like a man would.

She and I had several phone conversations with each other. She would text me pictures of herself. My mind was filled with her beauty and my desire to be with her grew. During one particular phone conversation, she led me into her bedroom, removed her clothing, and asked me to watch. My excitement grew, and I began to do as she did. It felt right. It felt damn good. That's how sin will do you. Makes the wrong look right and feel like silk on your soul. She did the unbelievable next. She brought our man into the scene, and I watched and listened to them make love in the bed. They called my name. They beckoned me to join them in this revolution of love. I just stood frozen. And then I just hung up the phone. If I had any innocence left in my life, it was gone at that moment. The thoughts and images running through my mind would not stop. What did I just open up my mind to? Could this be what God wanted me to do and be? I had always wanted to know what it was like to be with another woman. And I wanted an upright and understanding Christian man in my life. A two-for-one special! I could have my cake and eat it too. They both told me they loved me, wanted to marry me, and raise our kids together, and run off to where polygamy was accepted and live out our lives. Yeah, that's where I pulled the plug. Not when I should have—when I found out that another woman was involved—but just now, when marriage plans were revealed. What kind of sick mind did I really have? And, why wasn't anyone around me picking up on this? I was a member of a spirit-led, prophesying, speaking-in-tongues, casting-out-demons church. And not one prophet, evangelist, deacon, or pastor could pick up these evil spirits that had infiltrated my mind, body, and soul when I went up from prayer. So, I thought I was good. It was okay. God was okay with me like this. This was who I am. This had to be the reason why it was so easy for me to bring to this church the very man who just finished providing hours of oral sex on me before the watch night service and share a kiss at the stroke of midnight. There was a spirit there, but it was not the Holy Spirit. God loved me right where I was at, or so I thought.

PRIDE OF LIFE

Yes, this next man in my life was my savior. He was the one I reached out to after I had broken things off with the pastor and his fiancé. He swooped in like a tiger prowling on his prey. I knew he liked me for a long time, but I never gave him the time of day. He was a big man, not really my type, but he had a good heart, and that is why I reached out to him. The next thing I knew, he was driving me around in his Mercedes Benz, taking me on shopping sprees, and buying my kids anything and everything they needed or wanted. He told me he loved me and wanted to take care of me. He respected me and would never hurt me. He even purchased an engagement ring.

It is funny how money can make a person sexually attractive. Every stroke of his tongue on the inside of me made me even more hungry for that almighty dollar. I convinced myself that I was still a "good girl." Besides, I know plenty of women who use their "sex" as a tool to get money. Never mind they are called prostitutes. We were not engaging in "actual sex," just oral sex. He told me he wanted to but respected me and would wait until I was ready. I thought this was great! Goldmine! I struck gold! A man who finally respects me. Or, so I thought. Once again, that conviction inside me rose up, and this time, I listened, but not all the way. I broke it off, but not completely.

Not the way I was supposed to. I would later reap the consequences of holding on to what I thought was "a good thing."

LUST OF THE FLESH

A few years had passed, and I was trying to get myself together. I had landed an okay job, but knew it was going to be very temporary. But it did give me some time on my hands, unlike the rest. Enough time to meet the fourth man in my life. He was older but mature. Something I thought I needed in my life. Here was a man with a job, in the process of buying a home, and doing well for himself. He wanted to take me out of my parent's home and start a family right away. We found a house together, already picked out the kids' rooms, and had wedding plans underway. Life was good. Except for that nagging conviction that would not leave me alone.

What God? What do You mean this is not the man for me? He is a good man! He loves me. I know that he just got out of a divorce, but he says he is healed. He says he is ready. Yes, I know that he has pressured me into sex a lot, and I know that he is very, very persistent in knowing my whereabouts at all times to the point that it is annoying, but isn't that how a husband is supposed to be? Isn't that what love is?

Then it hit me. I really did not know what love was. Just look at all the men in and out of my life. I was searching for something I didn't know. I was searching in all the wrong places and in all the wrong people. I was looking for it in material possessions, the fulfillment of lustful desires, and what I thought was security. I was lost! So, I decided to end this relationship as well. Only this time, an event occurred that night that totally turned my world upside down. I became a victim of sexual assault.

All I remember from that night: I was silently screaming to God and reminding Him of the promises I had made to keep myself until marriage. All my efforts to get away were in vain as he held me down in a military style hold which kept me vulnerable and weak in every way. No one heard my verbal screams. My mind disconnected from my body, and I went limp. I remember that after he was done, he helped me put my clothes back on like nothing even happened. I remember walking aimlessly through a Wal-Mart that night, numb and nauseas. I remember getting home and taking a shower to wash away the stench of that awful night. I did not cry. I had no emotion. Little did I know that this night would germinate a seed that was implanted inside me long ago. That nasty little weed of unforgiveness.

Unforgiveness can turn a heart cold and bitter. It shuts out and turns down the voice of God. It can be so impenetrable to love, joy, peace, patience, kindness, goodness, faithfulness, gentleness, and self-control. I could not trust, would not trust any man. I made it a point to use men and lose them. Because that was all they are good for. I told God that I was angry at Him for letting this happen, and I had nothing else to say to Him at the moment. No man of God was worthy of my trust, and I was going to do this on my own. So, once again, I willingly picked up this shovel handed to me by the devil himself with a huge grin on his face, welcoming me back to the pit of despair.

I reached back to the "rich" ex-boyfriend of mine, but it was for nothing sexual, just business. He had a great monetary plan that would help him out and help me achieve the income I really wanted in life, only quicker and easier. Just sounds like a set-up doesn't it? Yeah, because that's what it exactly was. Here I was thinking I was going to make it big in five easy steps, but in reality, it was nothing but foolishness. Because I did not put my trust in God, ignored His voice, and put it all in me, a little "g" god. I brought on myself the lowest "lows" of my life: bankruptcy. Now how I started with an almost picture-perfect credit score where bankers were calling me to where I was ducking and dodging the sheriff car pulling up at my home was beyond me! But, it happened. And that ex-boyfriend who I thought was my "pet" had disappeared like a ghost, never to be heard from again.

Thank God for his goodness and mercy that I did not end up in jail and had nothing to be taken away by the creditors. Thank God that He had my hand all the way through it, even though I shook Him off. Thank God for His promises to never leave us or forsake us, even though we do it to Him. This whole process did not happen overnight, but over the years. And, over the years, God remained faithful, which opened my eyes once again. As I laid in my pit of despair dug by me for me with nothing but my thoughts, God spoke to me:

"Anna, listen to My words. I love you. I adore you. You are My creation. You are Mine. And I am yours. Don't forget My words, My promises to you. I will never leave you or forsake you. I have not forgotten you. I *have never left you. I have always been here. Waiting for you. Just waiting for you to make time for Me. I have specific instructions for you. And, I need all of you to receive them. Forget about everything going on around you. Forget about the men entering your life. What I have for you is more fulfilling and promising than what they offered. See Me and you will find Me. I am the love of your life. I am that void that you are missing. I am the great I AM. I am the One for you. Love is who I am, what you are missing, and I can be that for you. Abide in me, and you will see your eyes will be open. Enlightenment will be yours. You asked for wisdom; you will have it. Understand that it is yours. Insight you can have. Stay with Me, Anna. Don't leave Me. I have so much to give you. Stop worrying. I've got you. Trust me, Anna. Give it all to me.*

Habakkuk 3:6 (NKJV)

"He stood and surveyed the earth . . . " *(My life.)*
" . . . He looked and startled the nations . . . " *(My problems.)*
" . . . Yes, the perpetual mountains were scattered . . . " *(My problems, worries, and anxieties.)*
" . . . The perpetual hills bowed . . . " *(My past, history.)*
" . . . His ways are everlasting." *(His promises, His Word, never fails.)*

This is My word for you, Anna. Memorize it. Trust in Me. I've got you, Anna."

If that does not make you want to jump up and shout, then I don't know what will! God called me by name. He spoke to me! He said He loved me. He said that He is love! He said He adored me! He said seeking Him would help me find myself. Wow! That is the true meaning of love. That is what being close to the heart of Jesus means. He sees in me what I cannot. He loves me and wants to be in me. I repented and He forgave me! Just like that. No questions asked. No strings attached. And now He wants to draw even closer to me. I have no other desire but to draw closer to Him. I reached out of my grave, and He lifted me up. He uprooted that seed of unforgiveness that had attached to it bitterness, hate, lust, vainness, idolatry, and greed. I had learned how to forgive myself, those men who hurt me, and the countless others of my past and present. My life is my testimony. My testimony is God's love. God's love is amazing. All of this stuff should have driven me to the grave and sucked the living life out of me to a life of drugs, alcohol, promiscuity, and a physical and spiritual death. But God!

God kept repeating to me when He spoke, "Anna, I've got you." The same goes for you. No matter what kind of grave you have dug for yourself, no matter how big, how small, how wide, or how tall, you do not have to stay there. You do not have to be buried with all your sins. Jesus did that already. A man that knew no sin became sin for us on that cross. He was buried with all those sins of ours in the grave for three days. But what happened on that third day is the best part! He rose from that grave as the Savior of the world. He rose from that grave a holy and blameless God. God instructs us to be holy for He is holy. We will never be perfect like Christ while on this earth, but we can strive for perfection.

Look at my life. Perfect? Ha! Absolutely not! But I am trying. I will not give up my hope, my faith, or my trust in God. I will always keep Him first. I had to learn the hard way, unfortunately, in all my pride, ignorance, and arrogance. But I learned. And I will continue to give all that I am to God. This chapter will be forever closed in my life. A new chapter begins. The rose that was left for dead in the grave has arisen and is ready to grow in the light of God's Word.

Broken Pieces

❀ *The Valley*

The moment when you are sitting on the toilet, looking at the bare walls, and weeping, crying out to God to remove this feeling of emptiness, this darkness. Just asking that He touch your mind and heal it. It's the battle between mind and will.

Your eyes revert to the countless bottles of depression medications, pain relievers, antianxiety tranquilizers, and sleeping pills. *Maybe I should try them again. Maybe if I just take a lower dose, it will help me to get back to my normal.* But then the thoughts of dependency flood your mind. The thoughts of the day that you will have to come off those medications, and the wonder if you will be able to function without them. What is normal anyway? Normal seems overrated.

I used to know what normal was. I remember being happy at times. But as I remember only fragments of my childhood, they were not all very "happy" moments. I had more sad moments than happy ones. Was I ever normal? Was I ever happy? God, what is wrong with me? Can You please just heal my mind and give me joy, peace, and comfort? Please, God! I do not want to be like this anymore. I am so tired. *I am so tired.* Tears streamed down my face. Is God even listening? Of course He was. A warmth came over me, and I felt it in my chest. He was listening. He heard me. He reminded me that He is with me always and that He loves me. Even in the valley. Even in the shadows. Even in the darkness.

There are many of us who feel as though we have lived most of our lives in the valley, with a glimpse or two of the mountain's peaks. We have felt joy at some time in our lives. It was brief. But it was experienced. It was as though it was given in just the right amount so that we would not lose hope. So that we would not lose our faith. God gives us each a measure of faith. What is interesting is that just a mustard seed amount of faith can move mountains. So, what does that tell us about our own measurement? Are we that lacking? Yes. Yes we are. And that is why many of us stay in these valleys. Until we command that mountain to *move!* we will remain. And, in our remaining, we will build our faith. Because in order to stay on the mountain, faith must be established in our hearts and souls. It must be the foundation on which we stand unless we are shaken and fall a great fall. And suffer more than ever. This is why some of us stay longer in the valley. The mountain we must climb requires a great faith. Such a faith elevates us to become more like Christ and into a realm of insight that only God Himself can give to a willing vessel.

So, do not be discouraged in this valley. This valley has a purpose. This valley is planned. For God knows the plans for you. Do not be discouraged when those around you begin to elevate to their mountain. This means they have reached their measurement of faith and God will be able to use them at that level only. But you, you have a greater purpose. It is just like a pile of broken glass. Do you know what happens when glass is shattered? It is broken into hundreds of pieces, some sharp, some jagged, some large, some small. But do you know what happens when light hits those pieces? They glow with a rainbow of colors. Those of us who remain in the valley becomes shattered, broken, and worn. But it is not because we are bad people. It is because God must break us down—our will, our desires, our selves—so that He can shine even more through us when we climb to the top of that mountain. So that He is seen in our lives, not us. So that He alone is glorified.

So, take heart. Lift your head. It is not over. Do not be discouraged. Depression has no place in your life. Fear must not linger. Doubt must not stay. Sadness must leave. This is not the end. For even though we may walk through the valley, God is still with us every step of the way. Piece by piece, He is perfecting us, building our faith, and preparing us for a better future and hope.

WHILE IN THE VALLEY: GET RID OF FEAR!

Fear is the depletion of trust. The opposite of love. The divider of the faith. The destruction of a person's soul. Fear has many definitions. The most difficult concept of fear to accept is that its very presence in our lives means the very absence of God. The Bible says that perfect love casts out all fear (1 John 4:18). So, if we claim that Jesus is our Lord and Savior and that He is in our hearts, how do we continue to live in fear? Are we then really His?

Matthew 7:16 says, *"Ye shall know them by their fruits"* (KJV). Remember the fruits of the Spirit: love, joy, peace, patience, kindness, goodness, faith, gentleness, and self-control (Galatians 5:22-26). Why does love come first? Because love is God. Without love, none of the others will matter and/or can be obtained. Paul states in 1 Corinthians 13:2, *"If I have the gift of prophecy, and know all mysteries and all knowledge; and if I have all faith, so as to remove mountains, but do not have love, I am nothing"* (1 Corinthians 13:2 NIV).

Without love, we are nothing. We have nothing. Without God, we are nothing and have nothing. So, what creates a better cesspool for fear than a soul full of nothingness! Something has to occupy that space, and if it is not God and His love, then it must be fear. And, fear can wreak so much havoc on our lives. It creates mistrust, lust, hatred, and evolves into self-doubt, worry, and crushed hope. And without hope, we have nothing to live for and we die! This is the worse type of death. To be spiritually dead.

I struggled with fear. It held me down and suffocated my soul. It sucked the life out of me and made me feel worthless. It drove me to suicidal attempts, it drove me to lose my virginity before marriage, it drove me to have an abortion—it drove me to do things I said I would never do! Fear held me back from the promises that God had stored up for my life. I could not see past my current situation because its blinders over my eyes were so heavy. Its chains shackled me to people, places, and things that spoke death into my life, brought pain into my situations, and beat me down to the ground. Fear is powerful if you let it be. It will control you if you allow it to. And, until you are ready to break free and say you have had enough, you will never have your breakthrough. Until you realized that greater is He (Jesus Christ) who is in me than He that is in the world (1 John 4:4), you cannot overcome. Fear has no place in your life . . . *get rid of it!* Rebuke it in the name of Jesus. Speak the Word of God against it in Jesus' name.

> *"Even though I walk through the valley of the shadow of death, I will fear no evil, for you are with me; your rod and your staff, they comfort me"* (Psalms 23:4 ESV).

> *"For I know the thoughts that I think toward you, says the Lord, thoughts of peace and not of evil, to give you a future and a hope"* (Jeremiah 29:11 NKJV).

> *"For God hath not given us the spirit of fear; but of power, and of love, and of a sound mind"* (2 Timothy 1:7 KJV).

> *"For I am the Lord, your God, who takes hold of your right hand and says to you, Do not fear; I will help you"* (Isaiah 41:13 NIV).

> *"For we wrestle not against flesh and blood, but against principalities, against powers, against the rulers of the darkness of this world, against spiritual wickedness in high places"* (Ephesians 6:12 KJV).

> *"Be strong and courageous. Do not be afraid or terrified because of them, for the Lord your God goes with you; he will never leave you nor forsake you"* (Deuteronomy 31:6 NIV).

> *"The Lord is my light and my salvation— whom shall I fear? The Lord is the stronghold of my life— of whom shall I be afraid"* (Psalm 27:1 NIV).

> *"The Lord is my helper; I will not be afraid. What can man do to me?"* (Hebrews 13:6 CSB).

> *"Peace I leave with you; my peace I give you. I do not give to you as the world gives. Do not let your hearts be troubled and do not be afraid" (John 14:27 NIV).*

> *"For to be carnally minded is death, but to be spiritually minded is life and peace" (Romans 8:6 NKJV).*

Speak these verses over and over in your life. And once that spirit of fear has left, ask the Spirit of God to fill that void that it may never return. Trust and believe that you will know when that ugly spirit of fear has left because you will have that love you have been seeking, you will have that joy you have been missing, that peace that surpasses all understanding, that patience that can never be obtained in your own strength, more kindness to yourself and others, goodness overflowing in your words and actions, the gentleness of a lamb, and self-control that was out of control in your life! I have heard it said by my fellow military personnel that pain is weakness leaving the body. Well, I say redemption is fear cast out of our life and our souls! Your redemption is near! Cast out the fear in Jesus' name! Amen.

FAITH IS NECESSARY

Many of us have read Ephesians 6 and remember its reference to the armor of God. It is one of my favorite chapters as it contains powerful scripture to guard ourselves against the enemy. I would like to look at verse 16 of this chapter and share what God has shown me about what faith is, why it is important, and why it is a necessity in our walk through the valley.

Ephesians 6:14-17 (NIV) says, *"Stand firm then, with the belt of truth buckled around your waist, with the breastplate of righteousness in place, and with your feet fitted with the readiness that comes from the gospel of peace. In addition to all this, take up the shield of faith, with which you can extinguish all the flaming arrows of the evil one. Take the helmet of salvation and the sword of the Spirit, which is the word of God."*

It is *vital* that we first look at the order in which these four pieces of the armor have been listed in this verse because this is a game-changer. Within the duration of your walk, you need to have and know the **truth** in order to have **righteousness** in order to be **ready** to carry out your **faith**! Powerful! Let it sit in your soul for a minute.

Find it in your Bible and highlight it.

Truth = Righteousness = Readiness = Faith

So, what is faith? Faith is complete trust and confidence in someone or something. Hebrews 11:1 says *"Now faith is confidence in what we hope for and assurance about what we do not see."*

Faith is what opens the door to our understanding and blocks the arrow of doubt and confusion that the enemy throws at us.

Faith is our protection. It protects our spiritual walk and lives even in the midst of the trials and tribulations (flaming arrows). If we leave our faith, then we leave God's protection. First Peter 1:5 says *"Through faith we are shielded by God's power until the coming of the salvation that is ready to be revealed in the last time"* (NIV). This is why the helmet of salvation comes next in Ephesians 6. Because, without faith, there is *no* salvation!

So how do we build our faith? By studying His Word. Through prayer. And through fasting. Romans 10:17 says *"Consequently, faith comes from hearing the message and the message is heard through the word of God."*

Faith is like a muscle: it is only going to get stronger when you exercise it. The more we fast, the more we pray, and the more we read God's Word, the more powerful we become in our spiritual walk with Christ, and the more of a threat we become to the enemy—hence the shield! Amen!

BROKEN IN BODY

There are voices and images that haunt me.

Voices of a little boy who would hold me down and push his tongue in my mouth while playing "house." He would tell me I was the "wife" and he was the "husband" and he would not let me off the floor until I kissed him.

Images of a huge drunken Marine who put his fingers inside me as a teenager in the back seat of a car while I froze in fear and began to shake like a leaf until he saw that I did not enjoy it.

Images of the man that was supposed to love me rape me when I physically could not defend myself due to being in so much pain after a major car accident. The voice of the same man who told me it was better to have an abortion because he already had a child and did not want another one at the time, not knowing at the time that he just had another baby born by another woman. The images of how much I bled, screamed, and cried in pain for days alone during and afterward.

Images of a fellow airman who dragged me across a field to his barracks while onlookers did or said nothing . . . how I barely escaped his drunken threats. Images of how I woke up naked in my own barracks bed with barely any recollection of what happened, and a stranger lying next to me. The voice of a man who took advantage of my vulnerability and raped me and told me I could not say "No."

Images of me screaming and crying in my bed at night because of the contractions I had while pregnant with my second child, paralyzed in pain and unable to reach my phone, and my husband never home to comfort me or take me to the hospital.

Images of another man who pinned me down and stuck his finger and tongue inside me forcefully and with every scream of "no," he yelled "yes."

The voice of another man who blamed me for "killing" his baby because I miscarried. The same voice of that man who got angry and belittled me because he could not take advantage of me like I had let other men in my past.

The voice of another man who thought it was "cute" the way I tried to squirm away from him after telling him I did not want to have sex with him because I was saving myself for marriage.

These are the images and voices that make my body cringe. These are what made it difficult to show physical affection. This is what broke my body into pieces.

BROKEN IN SPIRIT

There is a lot about a person you will never know by looking at them. There are things that you will never discover without talking to them. I am one of those people. I am quiet, reserved, and not among the crowds. But, if you were to approach me, befriend me, just ask me if I am okay. You will find that beyond my smile is a story —a story of struggle, fear, regret, achievement, and faith.

I think my greatest wake-up to the reality of life was when I had an abortion at the age of eighteen. I knew better. I was raised in the church (woe to any church who supports this and does not speak up against abortion). I knew it was wrong. In fact, it was one of the things I said I would never do as a young lady. I had standards for myself, high standards at that. I had goals and dreams. I had it all figured out. But then, I was introduced to something that I did not plan. Life.

Life does not play by your rules. Life is also different when you leave the protection of your parent's house. It becomes, well, complicated and unpredictable. I left home as soon as I could to join the military. Everything was great! Then, I met a boy. A boy who became my whole world. I would do anything for him, to keep him, even murder. And that was how I found myself laying on the table, legs open, my mind cloudy, no emotion, no nothing.

I felt alone. I felt shame. I felt guilt. I felt dead. I wanted to scream, but I was so numb. I wanted to change my mind, but I was frozen in fear. Like something just sat on top of me and held me down, covered my mouth, and told me to "shut up" and take it like a woman!

I wanted someone to hold my hand, but no one cared. I was just another patient who was getting rid of their "problem." My mind flooded with ways to make this right. It was like I split in two, the good me and the evil me. It was my choice, right? I was young, not ready for a baby. I was just getting started in life. Besides, he said he already had a child and was not ready for another one. So, this was the best choice. He knew girls that got one and they moved on with their lives. He would even take me. He was there for me. Lies!

How I wish someone was there to stop me. How I wish someone could tell me I had options. How I wish someone could have just held me up right there before I opened up those doors of that clinic, so they could tell me not to do it. Where was that someone? I was looking for a sign, anything to tell me to turn around. I blacked out and woke up again, lay bleeding on a recovery table. My baby was gone. That was it. I could move on with my life, right? Wrong.

What came afterward is something that I would never wish on any woman on this earth. That is the constant reminder for the rest of your life that you killed an innocent human being. You may think that you will forget it, but your body never forgets. Your subconscious mind never forgets. There were days that I wanted to commit suicide. Days that depression set in around the timeframe of the incident. Days that when a friend tells you that she is considering an abortion, you burst into tears. Days that a baby commercial comes on the television, and your mind goes back to those horrid images. Days where a certain smell of blood will take you back. And, let me tell you something: a woman that is "shouting" the loudest about her abortion in this "shout your abortion" culture is really hurting the most.

Pray for her. Reach out to her. She is not okay. The emotional and spiritual hurt is very real. The aftereffects of your first "kill" is very real. I have forgiven myself now. I have given myself grace. And I know that God has forgiven me and has given me grace. I am doing better and take things a day at a time. I have even given her a name. I know it was a girl; I felt it. I have become pro-life and fight for all life, no matter what.

Because the pain after that *choice* is something no one can prepare you for. There is something that changes inside you after your first intentional murder of innocent blood. Your spirit begins to break and crumble. Your heart begins to harden, encapsulated by profound guilt and sorrow. You become desensitized to sympathy and empathy. Your outlook on life becomes dim and dark. The concept of a loving, merciful God begins to look entirely foreign as your sense of self has been destroyed, difficult to understand or to believe. You begin to feel that you can never be forgiven and deserve death, and deserve nothing good in life ever again.

But something changed that for me. I remember lying in bed one night, and this ugly-looking demon entered my room, sat on my chest with so much pressure that I began to sink, placed his hands over my nose and mouth, and began to suffocate me. I remember kicking and screaming for my life, trying to move his hands away so that I could breathe! I was scared to literal death, and I realized that I did not want to die. I deserved it, but I did not want to! With tears running down my face, I cried out the name of Jesus, Jesus, Jesus, but for some reason, my cries only caused this demon to laugh at me and mock me.

I was reminded that I did not believe I deserved to live, or the name of Jesus. I tried to quote the little pieces of Scripture that I knew, but this demon laughed at me even louder and reminded me that I did not even read my Bible. Feeling so scared and depleted, I did the only thing I could think of, and that was sing the childhood song that was wedged in the last part of my soul:

Jesus love me this I know, for the Bible tells me so, Yes Jesus loves me.

Repeatedly I sang it, and over and over it began to resonate in my soul. It was then that the demon began to tremble, loosen his grip, and yell at me to *shut up*, but I just sang louder and louder, with hot tears running down my face until that demon disappeared just as quickly as he came. Not today, Satan! Not tomorrow! Not ever! This is only part of my beginning and, by the grace of God, nowhere near the end of my life story.

I pray that this insight into my life story will help someone whoever thinks that abortion will solve their "problem." It may be a temporary solution, but it comes with long-term effects. This decision led to other horrible life choices due to my low self-esteem, depression, suppression of my true feelings, sexual abuse, divorce . . . etc. The fight in me left for a while. But thank God for Jesus! He has made me an overcomer and a silent whisper of hope for those who are going through. So if you walk by and see me smiling, just know that I smile because of what I've been through and how I am still making it!

❀ *Healing Is a Process*

Healing does not come overnight. Some wounds are deeper than others. Sometimes the scab is picked off and it makes the process longer. Sometimes the wound gets infected and the process has to start all over again. This is where the frustration comes in. This is where total reliance on God becomes vital. Over and over again, God would have to remind me of who He was and that He was always there for me.

My love language is words of affirmation. He knows how I needed to hear from Him and exactly what I needed to hear. He knew that I needed to hear things on repeat, and the best thing is that He never got tired of it! Here are some of the very words that God directly spoke to me over the years that hopefully can bless and encourage you during your healing process:

Anna,

You are My child in whom I am well pleased. You have found favor in my sight. I have tried you and found you true. I have tested you and found you worthy. Your time is coming. All that you have asked for will come to pass. Stay in prayer and continue to fast. Worship more, worship harder. I want to hear from you. Cry out to Me, the Lord your God. I love you and want to do so much for you. Just ask Me, your Daddy. Like you say, your Big Daddy. Anna, you are My love, and I want to be closer to you, more intimate with you. Let Me closer. Get to know Me even more. Let's fall in love all over again.

Forever yours,
Jesus,
Abba Father.

Stop worrying. My ways are higher than yours. My thoughts are greater than your thoughts. I am God. I control everything: the thoughts and the ways of man, I control. You are under My protection. Nothing will harm you. Take coverage under Me. You are where you need to be. Just rest in this place. Because greater things are coming. And you need the strength for what's to come. It's not a physical battle, but spiritual. You will be tried and tested. I want to know how much you want what you are asking for. Do I truly have all of you, Anna? Or is it lip service? I know your heart. I see your heart. And I know that you truly love Me. Keep seeking after Me. I love having your attention. It makes Me happy, Anna. Your attention makes Me happy. That is the way to My heart. I love you. Psalms 103:4-5.

I am God, and I am in control. I created time. Before you were even thought of, I was. Before he was even thought of, I was. Wait on Me. Wait on My timing. Don't let circumstances dictate to you what I am able / not able to do. I see all and know all. There are no imperfections in My planning. Trust in Me. See Me out for step-by-step instructions. Seek Me first and all My righteousness. Then everything will be added to you. My ways are not your ways. My thoughts are not your thoughts. My timing is not your timing. Have faith in Me. Rely on Me. I am your source. Take my lead.

Daughter, I have not left you. You are My child. I love you. You are precious. Trust in Me. Rest in Me. Leave all the fear and doubt behind. Rest in me. Take My hand. I missed you. I missed our conversations. Follow Me. Open your heart and mind to Me. I will show you the Way, the Truth, and the Life. Wait on the Lord. I will renew your strength. For My ways are not your ways. My thoughts are not your thoughts. Trust and believe in Me, and not on your own understanding. Hear My voice and believe. Hear My voice and trust. Hear My voice and obey. Only then will you be able to see all that I have in store for you. Make time for me. Be willing to open to hear My voice. Remove all distractions. It's time for a change. It's time to work. It's time to grow. It's time to move. Be willing. Be obedient. Stay awake. Stay focused. Stay watchful. I am caring. You are not alone. Trust in me. Amen.

Anna, listen to me. I have heard your cries. I feel your pain. I hurt for you. I cry with you. But know that I love you. This is not punishment. This is a blessing. This is a reminder that I have life and gave it more abundantly. Your joy will return. You will laugh. You do not need to be ashamed. I have covered you. I love you. I forgive you. I am proud of you. You bring me joy. Your heart is pure. I see your intentions. I see your struggles, but know that I have a deep love for you. Stay with Me, Anna. I'm not going anywhere. As you have reminded Me. I have never left you nor forsaken you. I'm here. I love you. My grace has covered you. Do not worry and do not be afraid. Live in the promise. Love Me with all your heart.

Continue to study My Word. Let it lead you and guide you from this point on. You are learning and growing, and sometimes it does hurt. But it's okay. Because I'm here with you through it all. I will wipe your tears. I know that you cannot be perfect. And I know that it hurts you that even in your best efforts, you fail. I know because I made you. And I know that you will fail. But, I also know that you do not stay down, Anna. You are a warrior. A fighter. Strong in your faith that will continue to grow. I need you to grow. I need you strong for what is about to come. Your family needs you, woman of God. So, stay praying. Stay in My Word. Stay true to Me. I will perfect you. I will honor you. I will hold you. Just stay steadfast in Me. Don't focus on your faults, your sins, or your downfalls because I don't. I see the woman you are growing to be. And I need you to see that as well. Be strong for your husband and your kids. Be strong in this battle called life. I am here with you always. Love, God.

Healing does not mean the pain goes away; it does mean that it no longer holds you hostage. As I heard this said once before: pain develops walls, but healing builds doors.

❀ Growth: I See What You Did There, God!

God only allows us to see the bits and pieces of the full picture. Why? Because that is the only way to push growth. If it was easy, everyone would do it. If we could all see the beginning and the end, we would all become self-righteous and have no need for God. If we knew all and could see all, we would be God. But, we are not, thank the Lord! I am thankful for this growing process. I appreciate God so much more through growth spurts. I am able to see what needs to be seen. Hear what needs to be heard. And do what God has purposed me to do. The pruning has begun. It hurts, but so worth it. God is clipping away the dead weight off my shoulders so that He can elevate me a little higher toward Him. My fruit is becoming sweeter, my leaves are filling with color, and my roots deeper. The direction I thought my life was heading has been shifted by the Son of Man who shines ever so brighter in my life. Away from the dark clouds of anxiety, depression, immorality, and most importantly, *fear.*

God's perfect love casts out all fear. I thought God moved me to another city to get married. But instead, it was to move me to my purpose. God will give you a place and a purpose before He brings a man into your life. It is in this place that you will grow. It is in this growth that you will find your purpose. It is in this purpose that you will find your faith. It is in this faith that you will see God. And when you can see what God is doing, baby, that is growth!

Do not get comfortable sitting in the same place. Comfort is not growth. Comfort is complacent. And when we are complacent, we forget God. We fill ourselves with pride and call our accomplishments growth. But, slowly, we are dying on the inside; our roots rotting, our fruit falling off, and eventually, our leaves wither. This is death. Something we all deserve. But thank God for Jesus, that He loves us and through His resurrection we can come back to life through Him. Amen.

Journal Journey Entries

ENTRY

I named her Deseree
And when she died,
She took me with her to her grave.
Her pain and agony, I felt.
Her tears and sorrow, I cried.
"Why did you not love me? Care for me?
Was I not good enough for you?
What did I do wrong?
Please tell me, and I will never do it again."
I took her cold hand in mine.
And cried even more.
She was cold, lifeless.
"I apologize," I said. "I didn't know what to do.

I was young. I was dumb.
I was ignorant. I was a fool.
I chose my life over you.
So stupid, I know.
I will never forgive myself.
In fact, I only know one solution,
And that's to end it."
As I reached for my knife and closed my eyes,
Ready to slit my own wrist,
Someone touched me.
I felt warm, renewed, and radiant inside.
My tears dried and my smile regained.
I opened my eyes and saw Deseree,
With a man glowing beside her.
"I forgive you, mom, and so does He.
Don't end your life this way.
I hope to see you in heaven one day.
I'll pray for you in eternity."
In an instant she was gone!
And, I woke up in my bed.
The pain was still there,
But I smiled.
Her name was Deseree.
And she was mine.
I will see her in heaven.
And together we will live forever.
Forgiven.

ENTRY

"People do not understand how powerful and influential music can be. Just take a moment to pay attention to what you are listening to and what kind of thoughts, memories, and actions come into play. We are created to worship, and depending on what we are listening to, we are either worshiping God or worshiping self, lust, greed, promiscuity, death, hell, or the grave. I will never forget the experience I had after being introduced to a ministry series by Pastor Craige Lewis called *Truth Behind Hip Hop*. It convicted me and changed my life forever! At the end of the series, I took my whole collection of music CDs and one by one, broke them in half. With each broken CD, it felt like demons were literally flying out of me and the heaviness on me was lifted with each *snap*. The CD I loved the most was the hardest to break, but once it was done, the largest weight was lifted. I just remember crying and shaking uncontrollably afterward. I didn't truly understand everything that took place that night, but something in me changed, and I would never be the same from that night on. Be careful of what we let into our spirit through the songs / lyrics we listen to. It really does matter. It is not "just music."

ENTRY

Dear God,

It seems like everything is happening so quickly in my life. I closed my eyes just for a quick second, and it seems like time just took off. I cannot believe that I am pregnant now, just got married, and will soon be off to Florida. What is going on? Regardless, I know everything is going to work out. I just cannot see it, but that is why I am putting it all into Your hands. There is no way I'm going to ever try to fix things to the way I think that they should because we both know how those events turned out. I just pray that You will give me faith, wisdom, courage, understanding, and peace that surpasses all understanding to make it in this life and time. I am not going to lie: I am scared. I am scared of this whole marriage and pregnancy thing. I never had to depend on anyone or take care of anyone to this extent but myself, and now I am going to end up doing both at the same time. My life has changed from here on out and it seems like my mind has now caught up with reality. I am no longer accountable for myself, but for two other people. I have my own family now.

Amen.

(Age 21)

ENTRY

Dear God,

. . . I pray that you will keep this baby alive, healthy, and kicking like he is now. I have him listening to gospel music now. Lord, he is such a blessing, and I thank You for him. I love him so much and pray that he will grow up to love and live for You. And that's why I dedicate this baby to You, Lord. This was such a surprise that I got mad and frustrated at first. But now, I'm in love and know this is truly a blessing and a joy to have kids and to have the ability to bear children. So, thank You, Lord.

Amen.

ENTRY

Dear God,

My life has completely changed. I am a wife and I just recently became a mother. So unbelievable! Thank You for a nice speedy delivery. It was painful, but You gave me a strong will and mind to get through. Even though neither my parents or my family was there to be by my side, You were there the whole way through. So, thank You. And even though my stay at the hospital was longer than anticipated because of my illness, I still thank You for it. I would not have learned as much as I have about the changes going on with my body and with my little son. All this made me a stronger person. Satan tried to hold me down with depression and hopelessness, but I know that You take care of your own. I started feeling better . . . no chills, no aches, no pains . . . I even learned my breasts respond to my son's cries. It is so weird! This has been the toughest obstacle in my life, but I learn and know that if I stay in Your will, You will make that mountain an ant hill . . . I ask that You will give me the wisdom that I need to become a good wife and mother. Love You and thank You.

Amen.

ENTRY

Dear God,

I am in complete shock . . . I do not understand . . . how am I going to afford all this? . . . I do not know whose plan this is, sure was not mine. I just cannot believe it! I took the home pregnancy test last night and my heart just sank. It had to be wrong . . . I called my sister-in-law and just cried. I do not know about doing this pregnancy thing again, Lord. Do I have it in me? Can I handle two young ones at once? Man, I thought I was just getting it together! Lord, please help me. I cannot do this without You. All my strength comes from You only. I need You now more than ever. Please help me to sleep tonight. And please take this nausea away. I cannot stand it. And I was thinking it was stress! Lord, please help mend me and my husband's relationship because it is not the greatest either. A lot of work needs to be done and it starts with You. Help him to realize that. He cannot do this on his own. He needs You in his life, God. Bless us and keep us . . .

ENTRY

This pregnancy was most definitely unplanned, and I was not even near ready to have another one . . . financially, mentally, or physically. But this pregnancy has taught me a lot: that God has a plan for our lives and we have *no* control over what He has in store for us. All I see is the downside to it, but He sees the bigger picture and knows that I can handle it. And I can. I have slowly been accepting it. So, He is wheeling and dealing in my life, and I just have to trust Him. I pray that I will be able to love my son the same after this one is born and learn how to divide my attention equally. Lord, I am going to need Your help!

ENTRY

Dear God,
This morning I threw up for the first time. I was not very fun. It was right after I ate some eggs and toast with my son. Yuck! Yesterday's baby shower was so much fun! I needed that kind of time out, even though I did have my son with me. It was nice just to get out of the house and have some fun without worrying or getting upset about stuff. And today's message was pretty good too. You keep reminding me that You have a purpose for my life, so I am praying that I will know what it is and do it with a grateful attitude. Lord, I pray for this family, just has a lot of bad spirits lurking around. I cannot do or say anything to change my husband's views on life because he only knows what he has grown up in, which was a broken home, and that is what he is trying to bring here. I can't do anything but pray for him. And God, I need You to help me out too. This pregnancy is hard, and I have all these crazy emotions! Just help me to keep them under control and help me not to worry or stress. Help me to have faith in You. You are in control. You make no mistakes. So, help me God. Help me, help me . . .
Amen.

ENTRY

Dear God,

. . . I broke down in my staff sergeant's office today. Man, I was so embarrassed. All I wanted to talk to him about was the call schedule and how it was going to work with me being pregnant. And then all the sudden, I started to just bawl my eyes out. Thank You, Lord for some understanding people surrounding me at this duty station. They are probably going to take me off the call schedule and make sure I get some time to make my appointments and whatever else I need to do. So, hopefully they will do that for me. But man, I am having it kind of rough this pregnancy. I am sick, tired, tired of being sick and tired. My house is a complete mess . . . this family and marriage needs some serious fixing. I am about to give up . . . help me, please.

Amen.

ENTRY

Childbirth and motherhood is so hard, but it is very rewarding. If someone is ever thinking of having multiple kids and worry about sharing your love, don't. It is natural. You will love the new baby just as much as the other child.

ENTRY

Now I have two to take care of: two car seats, two different types of diapers, two different personalities! I am trying to get used to it, but it is very hard and stressful. My son takes to her well, but now he is so whiny and clingy. Sometimes, I want to cry. Plus, my husband is no help at all: always hungover or nowhere to be found when I need him. So, I am stressed. But God is good, and I know He sees my pain and will take care of us.

ENTRY

Dear God,

I just got passed up for promotion again. But my friend made it, and I am so happy for her. She wanted it so bad . . . .so that means I will most likely be getting out of the military next year . . . I am tired . . .

Amen.

ENTRY

Well, today I finally see a little light of hope in this dark tunnel. I emailed my Chaplain, and she wants to sit down and talk with us, or just me if my husband does not want to. So, I am very happy that You have opened that door for us. I do not know where my husband is tonight, but I pray that he is out of harm's way and is okay . . . thank You. Amen.

ENTRY

Dear God,
. . . it is now 9:27 p.m. Where is he? He left around 6:30 p.m. This is what I'm talking about . . . But it's alright. I'm getting some help, whether he wants it or not. I am going to find some way to speak with my Chaplain. I have my supervisor involved, and she is going to talk with my master sergeant about getting me some time off to make it to some sessions. Because I am on the verge of leaving and never looking back. I am fed up and through. I am tried of his mom being involved . . . he is a grown man and he needs to grow up . . .
Amen.

ENTRY

Dear God,
. . . I think things are starting to look up. My husband began to read the book I read over the power outage day we had not too long ago, and he began to realize what he has been doing wrong and why I am so mad all the time. He actually took some initiative and actually was sincere on making everything work. He did it; not me. And that just blew me away. I just cried. It is the best thing that has happened between us since my son was born. I pray things only get better and we learn to speak each other's love language more often. I believe my "love tank" is beginning to slowly fill up. Maybe it's just beginning to become lubricated, but at least it is something. It all won't happen overnight, but something is happening, and I thank You, Lord for that . . .
Amen.

THE 4C HEART: Curls, Kinks, & Knots of My Dry, Thirsty, Single Soul

ENTRY

Dear God,

... I went to see my Chaplain. I felt so much better talking to her about things. I felt so relieved. My husband is going to have to come, though, to get the help we need. I still have my feelings of leaving only because I really do not see it getting any better. You have to want to make it work in order to see some progress, and it has to come from both sides. So him not making any effort to go to counseling to me is discouraging and so I really do not care to make any more progress. I know this is not the right attitude, so please help me. I am very discouraged, frustrated, and regretful that I ever got married. I just do not want to go on. So, please help me. Thank You for your blessings. Thank You for everything...

Amen.

ENTRY

Dear God,

Well, here I am again: praying, praying, praying. I started my "no television" fast last week, and I really hope that you have been listening to my requests. I have so many issues going on in my life and they are all very stressful on me. I took some leave this week, and hope that I will be able to rest up some and get things done...

Amen.

ENTRY

Dear God,

Yesterday, last night, I went off! I questioned my husband about all those profiles and numbers. Who is Celine? Who is Lavoria? Who is Lindsay? And, he had the nerve to laugh at me, call me crazy, and say "I'm trippin." He thought it was all a game. So, what did I do? Grabbed the nearest suitcase and started packing up his stuff. I sure did... It wasn't funny then. I threw all his clothes out the closet! I was not playing. I was so angry that I was shaking. You surely did intervene by having my sister-in-law call right in the middle of it because if she did not, I would have thrown him out in the streets! I do not know what came over me, but I just could not take him looking me straight in they eye and lying about everything. And, just smiling about it... but God, You stepped in right on time and spoke some words of wisdom through her. I truly needed to calm down, get a grip, and just pray. All we were doing was crying out for help from each other in our own separate ways: my husband goes to women, and I just lock everyone out and stay to myself . . . .He is still wrong for reaching out to other women, lying about not having a wife or kids . . . just putting himself out there as available, period. He would not like it if I did it. So why is it okay for him? My husband had no response to that question. Interesting. So, Lord, I am still praying and fasting . . . I am still hurting, Lord. And I need Your healing physically and emotionally . . .

Amen.

ENTRY

Dear God,

. . . I am so exhausted, so I am going to bed . . . I am so angry, and I have been doing and lifting things I should not have, but who else was there to help me? . . . I did not help my husband put away the clothes I packed up out of his closet, so he gets mad and tells me he is not going to help me around the house, threatens me with bad karma, which I told him that I do not believe in that, so then he tries to bother me by flicking on and off the lights, turning up the music to my radio, banging the bed, just making as much noise and being as much of a nuisance that he thought he could be, and then left out leaving the lights on in the room. Lord, I really had to pray because I knew it was just the devil. That is all that was. So, I just really need an answer. Should I stay and put up with this foolishness? Or, should I leave and let him figure it out on his own? I cannot live like this too much longer. I am physically worn out. My heart is hurting. I need help, God.

Amen.

ENTRY

Dear God,

. . . I'm in the hospital with my son because he came down with a really bad upper respiratory cold and had to stay with him overnight in the medical-surgical unit (MSU). Help me, God, because I need it really bad. My patience is running thin, and my willingness to stay in this relationship is on thin ice. So, keep us in Your thoughts. God, watch over this family. Especially this little one in my womb.

Amen.

ENTRY

Dear God,

... Still hanging in there. I am just praying this baby can hang on until my due date. She is trouble, trouble, and impatient. After this one I am *done*. No more. They say no pregnancy is ever the same, and they ain't never lie! This is the complete opposite of my son. Went from no problems with a very active baby inside me to having all the problems with a laid-back baby! Until recently, I have been having contractions out of this world with her. They had to give me some type of medication to slow them down. What is her hurry? I am even on half days at work, which is lovely! I'm not complaining about that part! My Christmas was nice. My mom (returned home from her deployment) and my grandma got to see my son for the first time! It was fun! Thank You for everything ...

Amen.

ENTRY

Dear God,

... for right now, I want to see what goes on in counseling and if it is going to help. Maybe everything will turn around for the both of us. But if not, I still love him but will move on. Not divorce, but separate. I will sell the new car I am driving, find a job with benefits, have my family help me out with the kids, and start a new life without him until he finally decides to grow up and be a man. So, we will see. It is all lifted and given to You, Lord ... Amen.

ENTRY

Dear God,

I feel so lost with my son being gone to stay with my parents for a while. There is so much time, I have no idea what to do with it. It is amazing how much of my time and energy went into him. Thank You for letting it happen. This marriage needed it, my daughter needed more of my time, and I needed it for myself. My daughter is loving it and is just trying to talk and holding her head up, and she is only two months! She is smiling and is just a blessing. Thank You. Keep

my son safe with my parents and family. I pray that he will not forget us and will continue to hold us dear in his heart. Thank You, Lord.
Amen.

ENTRY

I worry that I will have to raise these kids on my own, but I trust in God to pull through for me.

ENTRY

Dear God,
. . . I am just curious to find out how all this is going to work out. I am just tired, burnt out, and very hurt, and do not want to take it anymore . . .
Amen.

ENTRY

Dear God,
Well, the countdown begins, and I am praying that you will just lead the way to greatness. I am doing this dinner fast until I hear a "word" from You . . . I did not rank up again, which means my girl made it and I am so glad for her. I am more excited than worried about what the future holds because I know that You are in control. That is all I need. I can smile again. The world tells me that I am making a big mistake to leave the military, but God, who are they? They cannot see any further into my future than I can. You are the beginning and the end. In You, I put my trust. Lord, I love You and know You have it all under control. My marriage has gone downhill, my son is still gone, my car has not sold yet, and I am waiting for some good weather to do a yard sale. I lift all these concerns and more to You. You know my heart, my desires, and not my will but Yours be done. Thank you, Lord. I love You and praise Your name with a smile on my face.
Amen.

ENTRY

Dear God,

It has been three years. So much has changed for the better. After three years of separation (which my husband told me he spent dating other women to see if he even wanted to stay married to me and asked why I wasn't dating), my husband and I are divorced. He later ended up in jail for circumstances I was unaware of. I am still staying with my parents with my two kids, I have finished up my licensed practical nursing (LPN) program, and now working on my registered nursing (RN) license. It has not been easy: a lot of blood, sweat, and literal tears. But I have grown much in you, I am happier, I am full of life . . .

Amen.

ENTRY

During counseling today, this woman pastor shared with me something that for some reason was foreign to me. She told me she had never been sexually assaulted, never been touched inappropriately, and could not relate to any of the traumas that I shared with her. She apologized that I went through that. My brain went into shock. For some reason, I thought this was "normal." I thought every woman went through this. I thought this was expected behavior from every man. I really had a hard time believing her at first. And then, I began to question: why did I think this

way? What kind of warped brain did I have to think this was normal behavior? Was it the confusion that happens to a victim's brain when the boundaries of desire and disgust become muddled? This conversation with her has forever changed me. Seeds of self-worth were planted. Time to renew my mind in this area of my life.

ENTRY

Wow, God! As I look back through the pages of this journal, I can see that my life has been a bunch of ups and downs, ins and outs. And yet, You still love me! You have never left me or forsaken me. You have been so patient with me. I have been from one extreme to the next. From an ex-husband to a perverted pastor to my finances being held up. But you know what, God? I have noticed that through every situation, I always turned to You. I never lost my faith and trust in You. All these troubles and worries I placed on myself because I strayed away from You and Your truth. I put man over You, money over You, and myself before You. I have truly learned what the commandment that we should have no other gods before You means. It is not necessarily little graven images, but anything that takes Your time, Your place, and Your worship.

God, please forgive me. I understand now. I spoke a lot of things into my life. Those things that I spoke, I bind them up right now in the name of Jesus. For whatever we bind up on earth is bound up in heaven and whatever we lose on earth is loosed in heaven (Matthew 16:19). I loose blessings upon my life: financial, spiritual, and physical.

Father, You reminded me in Your work in Romans 8:28 that all things work together for the good of those who love You. Right now, I am standing on Your Word and that promise . . . God, I believe that there is nothing I give to You that You cannot fix . . . Erase my slate and build me, mold me, and shape me into the woman of God You truly desired for me to be all along. God, I am crying out to You to rebuild me. Tear down my strongholds that I built up against You, tear down my idols, and purge me with hyssop. Wash me whiter than snow. Create in me a clean heart. And renew a right spirit within me. Thank You, God, for Your joy and peace that surpasses all understanding. Open my eyes that I may see You more clearly. Open my ears to hear Your voice, open my heart that I may commune with You more. I love You, Lord. Thank You for listening to me. Amen.

ENTRY

I am frustrated when I am not in my Father's presence. It is the worst place to be.

ENTRY

Prayer cry:

I repeated the same mistakes. Just when I thought I had it figured out, I see myself crying, hurting, and ashamed all over again. Same story, different tune. I was lying to myself all along. My self-righteous act demasked. I failed God and myself. I failed my kids. I chose lust and lies over God. How can I show my face? I want to die. New life is growing in me, but I have no joy. I fell for the lie of a promise that has not been ful-

filled. Will it ever?

I feel duped, used, and abandoned once more. I worked so hard to work toward something that will never happen. I dreamed of a day that I will be happy and joined with someone who will love God and me and my kids, but does he? I am tired. I am so tired. I suck at life. Why can't I do the right thing? Why do I hurt myself? Why does God put up with me? I'm tired. What is my purpose?

I feel like all I do is mess up. I can't do anything right. I'm tired of crying, tired of worrying, tired of being unhappy, tired of me! I hate this flesh. It does nothing but mess up. I do nothing but disappoint the one I truly love. Jesus, I am sorry. I failed You once again. I tried to do it in my own strength, thought I was strong enough, but no! And the devil just laughs because I have fallen. I have been knocked down and don't want to get up. I'm tired. Tired of living this life. Why am I here? What is my purpose? No one knows my inner thoughts but You, God. I feel so far away from You. And it's my fault. I did this. I separated us because of my sin. I am so sorry. I want to make it right, but don't know how. I don't know how to fix this. I give You all my broken pieces. Help me, God! Please help me. I don't want to be here in this place again. This place of brokenness, regret, fear, anguish, resentment, anger, fatigue, and hopelessness. Give me hope, God. That's all I have. Give me peace, Lord. That is all I need. Fill me up, Lord, with love and forgiveness. I am relying on Your grace and mercy to survive. I am tired, broken, and heavy-laden. I just want to rest in You. Help me to rest in You. Carry me through. Help me to rest in You. May Your gentle waters flow through me and wash me clean. I am sorry, Lord. Help me to turn my life around. I need You more than ever. Thank You, Lord. I love You so much. Amen.

I am so glad that God does not take our words and take them out of context as we sometimes do with His words. So glad that He does not take our words and twist them into what He wants to believe about us. So glad that He knows our hearts and knows how we truly are. That is why He can understand us even when we do not have the words to speak. I am glad He does not use our words against us to point out our sins. So glad that He is a safe place for us to open up to without fear of backlash or judgment.

We can just pour out our hearts, our tears, our screams, our yells, our laughter, our doubts, our anger . . . etc. and know that when it is all said and done, He does not take it to heart, and loves us just the same. His love is so amazing, so limitless, so unconditional . . . it is too hard to explain in words. Thank You, Lord, for Your love. Thank You for Your grace. Thank You for Your mercy. Enough is enough is enough. This repeated cycle has to end, and it will end today! I surrender, and I move forward. God, You are in control! Take my life and use it for Your will . . . have Your way!

ENTRY

I could have died this year . . . twice. Brought in the New Year laying in a hospital bed clinging to life itself. They say it was a strange respiratory virus that a few young people had recently came in with, maybe it was double pneumonia . . . I just thought that I was under the weather and did not go into the hospital until it was at its worst. Is this a precursor of how my year was going to be? What was the meaning of this? I am too young for this, and to get it twice in one year? I do not understand, Lord. I have been trying to live right, live for you. Do I need to slow down? Take it easy? Take care of myself? But it is so hard! I am by myself . . . I need help! I have two teenagers now, and one of them has straight-up lost his mind! I do not know what to do. I am struggling. Everyone is giving advice but no solutions. Everyone is pointing the finger, but no one is lifting a hand. I know You are my kids' heavenly Father, but God, they need a physical father figure who is consistent and will be present. You said you sent someone to me? But God, he is older than me and he's a minister who lives in Atlanta. I do not want to move and live in Atlanta. And, don't you remember my history with older men, ministers, and especially preachers from Atlanta? You want me to love him and support him, and to be there for him for the rest of his life? Okay, all I can do is trust You. This heart monitor itches.

Please, God, I am in survival mode. All I can do is trust and believe in You. I can't see what you see, but I can try. Trust seems to be the motto of this year. Yes, Lord, I will trust the process. Yes, Lord, I say yes to Your way and Your will.

Amen.

ENTRY

Well, God, that relationship ended unexpectedly. Another relationship that was a lesson, but I'm glad I listened to You and was obedient even though it did not make sense. I feel as though I had one promise me marriage but never put a ring on my finger. I had another put a ring on my finger but could not bring me to the altar. The third time is always a charm, I guess! But I am very thankful for how You put a halt to everything before I uprooted my family. God, you expose the conditions of hearts—what is hidden versus what was presented. You exposed my heart, and You exposed his heart. Yes, it was hurtful to open up only to have those same hurts I shared happen all over again. But, thank You for covering me. Thank You for showing me that I am not as ready as I thought for marriage. I have things to work on. I have my family issues to work on. I have my self-worth to work on. I have my self-respect to work on. I have my self-esteem to work on. I need to say goodbye to the dust in my life in order to take my peace into my newness. I am more interested in pleasing You than man. I am searching for my fulfillment in you. I want more, God! I am searching for a higher level. I am not content being here. Romans 6:8 (KJV), *"For to be carnally minded is death, but to be spiritually minded is life and peace."* God, I want Your life and Your peace. I want to be surrounded by those who are truly Kingdom-minded. Thank You for placing me in a work environment with like-minded believers. They have truly been a blessing in my life. They have been an Aaron and Hur to my Moses, helping me hold my hands up in the midst of my battles (Exodus 17:12-14). God, you are not yet finished with me. There is so much more to do. And I am willing and ready. Help me not to get distracted. Help me not to get discouraged. Strengthen my faith. I will trust the process. I will be teachable in this wilderness. I will come out renewed and ready with the strength and courage to embrace Your will in all things and to renounce whatever is contrary to it.

Amen.

ENTRY

Ever scroll back through your timeline on a social media site, look through all your posts and pictures? It is amazing how much has happened in all those highlights of our lives. It reminds us of how quickly time goes by. Imagine if that is God's view of our lives. Just walking, scrolling timelines. And just like that, the timeline ends and there is no more! What did it all mean? Did you accomplish anything with purpose in this life? Did your timeline include others with love and respect? Was the love of Christ ever a part of anything we did?

The Bible says our life is like a vapor: here today, gone tomorrow (James 4:14). It's like a grass which the wind blows over, and its place remembers it no more (Psalm 103:15-16). We must live each day like this is our last. We must live with purpose. The way others who scroll through our timelines can be perfected and live even better than we ever did. Legacy is left, not lived.

ENTRY

Ever feel like the modern-day Job at times? I remember calling my sister one day complaining to her that I felt like him when I had a painful boil grow on my eyelid and found out that it got infected and would have to have a surgical procedure to remove it. I was at a point in my life that one thing after another had just been happening. I thought I found love but ended up breaking off that engagement. My son ran away from home, was found days later, and ended up in a mental health facility, then weeks later, was placed in a family friend's home because he did not want to return home, and then eventually went to go live with his father. My daughter's teenage hormones were kicking in, and she was having some temporary insanity moment, and do not get me started on that darn *Tik Tok*! Constant changes were going on at my job, and I was struggling to keep up and trying to decide if I was going to stay. As if that was not enough, had to get scheduled in my late thirties for my first mammogram because a lump was found in one of my breasts (do your breast self-exams and go get your physicals done, ladies). And, the dog, well, the dog was probably the only "normal" thing left in my life!

There were many nights I cried. I fell into depression, and I became suicidal. I felt like the worst mother ever. I felt like a failure. I struggled with balancing work life, home life, relationship life, my life—I had no life! What was the point of my life? I sat in my closet, lights off, beating my head against the wall, just staring at the safe where my gun was stored. I could end it now, and all my problems would go away. I have to do it in a way that looks accidental so my kids can still get the insurance money and be taken care of. And, then I get mad at myself again because I can't even attempt suicide without thinking of someone else. My thoughts race back to my childhood where I would cry in bed, begging God to take my life because I was so scared. Scared if I was going to face the wrath of my mom's short temper the next day. Scared of not knowing if my parents were going to stay together because all they did was argue and fight almost every day and night, the sounds of the screaming, yelling, and objects breaking as I pulled the pillow over my head trying to drown out the noise. I remembered my mother walked out one evening after an argument she had with my dad and said she was done and did not return for a day or two later. I remembered being slapped into kingdom-come because I shared my true feelings. All I wanted was someone to say, "Anna, I see you, I love you," and to hug me. I hugged myself in bed at night, tears streaming down my face, begging for God to take my life. It would be better that way. And, here I am, a grown adult, many years later, hugging myself in the dark, contemplating on helping God to deliver that same request. Why does death seem so inviting? So appealing? Even Job says: "*O that thou wouldest hide me in the grave, that thou wouldest keep me secret, until thy wrath be past, that thou wouldest appoint me a set time, and remember me! If a man die, shall he live again? all the days of my appointed time will I wait, till my change come*" (Job 14:13-14 KJV). I think it is because we feel as though it seems to appear as a hiding place. It looks as though it will protect us, conceal us, and preserve what we feel is the last little bit of good we have left. The only problem is that, my friend, is an illusion. Death is death. It is permanent. Your chapter on this earth ends. The only person who defeated death was Jesus. And since we are not Him, we won't be returning back to this earth after we die.

I am so glad that God did not answer those heartbreaking prayers of my childhood. I am so glad that I broke against the stigma against counseling and went to work on my mental health. This is so vital, especially, for those of us in the African-American community. We grow up with the most devastating command: "what goes on in this house stays in this house." How do we break the cycles of fear, sexual abuse/addiction, substance abuse/addiction, lust, and any other perversion if it is locked up and never talked about? If there is no freedom to speak? Many of us suffer in silence. It is time to break that silence. Go get help! It is not too late. There is nothing wrong with asking for help. Nothing wrong with opening up. Nothing wrong with having and showing emotion. It is okay to cry. It is okay to feel. It is *okay*! If you do not work on knowing who you are and finding your self-worth, your value, you will continue to let a lie tell you who you are and what your purpose is. Lies are the manipulators and con-artists of the soul, and they become the most powerful when you are vulnerable. It is time to be healthy and free. It is time to live out your purpose with a new heart, soul, and mind.

Unaddressed pain can become your personality. You do not have to become that past pain in your life. Pain should only be a visitor, not a tenant. Take care of your mental health. Take care of your spiritual health. Take care of your physical health. Take care of yourself. Those hurts do not define you. You are blessed. Your life does have value. You will *never* be perfect. No need to put that pressure on yourself. Just strive to be your best. When you do not value the place and space you are in right now in your life, you will have a hard time valuing where you will or could be in the future. Surround yourself with good company that will hold you accountable. Get under a good church ministry that will help prune and help you grow, not one that takes advantage of you, robs you, and leaves you hanging when you need them most. Do not be held down to manmade church traditions but led by the Holy Spirit's conviction. There have been many of us who have been hurt by the church, but we cannot use those experiences to forsake the assembly and give up on our pursuit and purpose of God's perfect will for our lives. Do we quit going out to eat all together if we have a bad experience at a particular restaurant? No, we just will not return, maybe write a bad review, and go try another place to eat. Finding a good church should be no different.

Church institutions are made up of imperfect people who can get it very wrong at times, including you. This is why it is so important to have a relationship with God yourself and to be in tune with the Holy Spirit. And, go find a church that does the same. Learn how to forgive and let go. Inhale. Exhale. Shake it off. And, let it go! God's got you. And He loves you very much. You will live and not die. You are God's child!

"Those who sow with tears will reap with songs of joy. Those who go out weeping, carrying seed to sow, will return with songs of joy, carrying sheaves with them" (Psalm 126:5-6 NIV).

THE 4C HEART: Curls, Kinks, & Knots of My Dry, Thirsty, Single Soul

ENTRY

God knows all, sees all.
Sees the heart.
Sees the sin.
Sees all that's covered.
Sees through the darkness.
Brings all the light.
He knows all.
He has created all.
There will never be a God like we serve.
There has never been like a God we serve.
Who has ever given their life
To save the world.
To save every sinner no matter their sin.
This God that I love is the lover of my soul.
No man will ever replace.
No man will ever take His place in my heart.
No matter the pain, circumstance.
I will praise my God.
I will give thanks.
I will give Him glory.
For all!
Because He is my God.
And I love Him with all my heart, soul, and mind.
Amen.

ENTRY

I am a promised child.
A child of the King.
For He has given me grace, mercy, and love.
He has given more than I asked for.
My cup runs over.
To share with others.
To bless others.
I am a promised child.
A child of the King.
I was given a purpose.
To live by faith

And share my faith
With those who have lost theirs along the way.
I am a promised child.
A child of the King.
I thank You, Lord,
For chasing me.
And giving me life everlasting.
Amen.

ENTRY

The time will come,
When I will call you,
And you will need to respond.
The days grow shorter because the end is near.
I need you to prepare yourself.
Fast, pray, and read My Word.
Study and show yourself approved.
Read My Psalms, My revelations.
Meditate on My precepts.
Cry out to Me, and I will hear you.
Cry out to Me, and I will respond.
The time is near.
And, the days are growing short.
I will be your God.
And you will be My people.
Cry out to Me.
And I will heal your land.
You must seek Me.
You must acknowledge who I am.
You must know that I am the Lord your God.
And I love you very much.
Amen.

References for this poem-
Psalm 65:4 (KJV)

Blessed is the one whom You choose and bring near to You to dwell in Your courts.
Revelation 14:12 (KJV)

Keep God's command and the faith of Jesus.
Matthew 26:41 (NASB)

Keep watching and praying that you may not enter into temptation; the Spirit is willing, but the flesh is weak.
Ecclesiastes 2:25 (NLT)

For who can eat or enjoy anything apart from him?
Song of Solomon 8:4 (HCSB)

Young women of Jerusalem, I charge you: do not stir up or awaken love until the appropriate time.
Job 4:17 (NASB 1995)

Can mankind be just before God? Can a man be pure before His maker?

ENTRY

"He shall be like a tree Planted by the rivers of water, That brings forth its fruit in its season, Whose leaf also shall not wither; And whatever he does shall prosper" (Psalm 1:3 NKJV).

ENTRY

Remember, the Lord is looking for those who desire Him. And for those who fear Him. Scripture reading from Nehemiah 1:6-11.

ENTRY

Sometimes we must go.
We must be moved from our comfort zone.
So that God can speak and be heard in our lives.
Brings us to lows, valleys, droughts,
So that we may be tested.
Brings us to His heart.
So that we may be sustained.
For God is a good Shepherd.
And we must trust His ways
Are the only way.
To life, to joy, to genuine happiness.
Lord, I trust You with my heart, my soul, my mind.
You are my gatekeeper.

I will be free in Your courts.
And, I will worship You.
All the days of my life.
Amen.

ENTRY

Words cannot express how I feel.
That brought death and destruction to mine.
But God has sustained me and covered me.
They brought disruption and confusion.
But, God has not settled me and protected me.
They cheated on me and hurt me.
But, God has healed me and made me stronger.
Thank You, Lord Jesus for this testimony.
Thank You for showing me You truly care.
Thank You for showing me You truly care.
Thank You for never leaving me or forsaking me.
Thank You, and I love You.
Amen.

ENTRY

There are four foundational core values that makes us valuable women of God: Jesus, love, knowledge, and prayer. We are nothing without Jesus. No husband, child, marriage, career, or finances can replace Him. We are nothing but noise if we cannot love (1 Corinthians 13:1). Learn to speak the love language of God in order to speak to the king and queen of others, and not bring out the fool. Remember that God knows our future today, so we can trust His knowledge and wisdom. Ask for it. And prayer is the direct access to the power of God. Have a prayer life that is constant and consistent so that God's will may be done on the earth as it is in heaven.

Amen.

ENTRY

"Seek ye *first* the Kingdom of God and all its *righteousness* . . . " (Matthew 6:33 KJV). What is righteousness? How do we obtain it?

James 3:18 (NKJV, emphasis added), "Now the _fruit_ of _righteousness_ is _sown_ in _peace_ by those who _make peace_."

Isaiah 32:17 (ESV, emphasis added), "And the _effect_ of _righteousness_ will be _peace_, and the result of righteousness, quietness and trust forever."

The answer: Righteousness is peace. Be peacemakers, beautiful women of God. Speak up in love. Stand up for others. Share your testimony with others. Establish a legacy of peacemaking in your children by teaching them to resolve disagreements through consideration and compromise. And most importantly, practice what you preach by living a life based on the principles of God's Word.

"Blessed are the peacemakers, for they will be called children of God" (Matthew 5:9 NIV). Our God is a "God of peace." And there really is no peace for anyone outside of Christ. So, in order to obtain righteousness, we must have peace with God and with each other.

According to Romans 14:17 (NIV), " . . . the kingdom of God is not eating and drinking, but righteousness and peace and joy in the Holy Spirit."

This is the Kingdom of God. This is righteousness. Let's ask God for the infilling of the Holy Spirit so that we can live in accordance with the Scripture. The understanding of the infilling of the Holy Spirit begins with a question, "Are you spiritually thirsty?" If you desire for a deeper relationship with the Lord, then you will start to understand why the Lord has given us His Holy Spirit.

Lord, we ask for Your love, joy, peace, patience, kindness, goodness, faithfulness, goodness, gentleness, and self-control. May we pursue the things that make for peace and mutual upbuilding (Romans 14:19). We renounce pride, self-reliance, and selfishness. Equip us to do Your will on this earth. Help us to serve with deep and happy confidence in You. May You rule and reign in our hearts, souls, and minds. Holy Spirit, quench our spiritual thirst and give us spiritual power to live for you.

Amen.

ENTRY

God gave us five things to establish before anyone partners with us:
1. Place. He places us where purpose can happen in our lives.
2. Purpose. God reveals purpose in your place. If you can embrace the place, you can then embrace the purpose.

3. Provision. God provides where He calls us to and He will fund His ideas and plans.
4. Identity. We are to be like God.
5. Parameters. Steps 1-4 must be in place. We must be willing to submit to the will of God. When the purpose of a thing is not known, abuse is inevitable.

Marriage does not improve but exposes your singleness. If you feel misplaced in your singleness, purposeless in your singleness, empty in your singleness, you will bring that into your marriage. A spouse cannot complete and fulfill you. You must already be in position, moving forward with purpose and direction so that the person who God places in your life will be able to support and encourage what has already been instilled. Your passions and callings will be his and vice versa. Having this in place before becoming one flesh will keep you and your future spouse from pushing against each other throughout your lives together. Exposure happens in marriage. May it expose a Kingdom woman of God with her mighty Kingdom man of God united in love and purpose.

Be purposeful in your singleness. Do not hang on to someone who is pulling you away and distracting you from your place and purpose that God has called you. You are *not* a ride-or-die chick. I remember my husband asking me to be this for him. Instead of agreeing, I should have been asking where were we were riding to? And telling him, "No, I am not interested in dying!" The same goes for you! Do not be afraid to let that brother know that what is in him spiritually transfers to you, and if it is not of God, you do not want in. Let him know that he may have everything that you like, but he has not let God take care of his insecurities. If he does not know his place, purpose, provision, identity, or parameters, how is he secure in how to lead you in those areas? Hold yourself accountable. Trust God. Trust the process.

ENTRY

Some of us have difficulty deciphering the real versus the counterfeit, and we risk following false products and loving a wolf. Women of God, we have got to establish a strong prayer life and walk with Christ Jesus. It is through those two things that discernment grows. Discernment is the ability to see beyond what is presented.

Our adversary the devil can present very well and will bait his hook very well, so we must remember that he is out to kill and destroy, and he does not believe in catch and release.

So, how can we tell if it is God or not? Always remember the following: God's words and ways always align with the Scripture. They never take you from Himself. They convict, which promotes change in yourself and promotes spiritual maturity, and there will always be repetitive confirmations.

Keep in mind that the enemy operates in confusion and chaos. He uses three counterfeits. The first is cured loneliness. Men, alcohol, drugs, sex, careers, degrees, kids . . . etc. will not cure loneliness for you. The cure for loneliness is not company but calling.

The second is your preference. The devil will send you pain gift-wrapped in your preference, but always remember that God never speaks our preference, only purpose.

The third is a shortcut. Satan will always try to show you the easier way out, present the five easy steps to greatness, or introduce an alternative route that may start out great but end in an utter mess. God does not use shortcuts, yet enjoys the scenic route.

We must trust the route of the wilderness. It is in the wilderness where we grow, mature, and find our calling and purpose. It is in the wilderness where our prayers will expose the hooks of the enemy. It is in the wilderness where our discernment is heightened and shortcuts are identified. And because our discernment has been heightened, our attraction has been corrected, and we no longer love wolves but the Good Shepherd, and we no longer love the false products but the truth of God's Word. Amen.

ENTRY

Woman of God, please remember that a man will protect what he values. Even so much more will God protect you. The perfect example of this is in Job 1:10. We see here that Satan is pointing out that Job is obviously all that God claims him to be because he is protected by a hedge around him, his family, and on every side.

But wait a minute, Satan. How did you know it was there? How did you know where it was placed? How did you know who it was protecting? What exactly have you been up to? Up to no good as usual. Thank You, Holy Spirit, for being the hedge of protection over our hearts, souls, bodies, and minds. Thank You, God, for keeping us from the seen and unseen attacks on our daily lives from the enemy. Help us to stay in Your Word and in Your way. Help us to remain prayerful. Thank You for sealing us with Your protector and hedge: the Holy Spirit within us. May we stay safe and whole in You.

Amen.

ENTRY

What I have learned is to make sure that I value myself as God values me. And, when I do, I will know the difference for when man violates and tries to devalue me.

- *No*, it is never okay for a man to touch you in any way you did not want. "No" means no at *any* time, *period*. This is sexual assault. Please report it. First Corinthians 6:19 says our body is the temple of the Holy Spirit, not for a perverse spirit who has no self-control.

- *No*, oral sex is not "safe" sex. You may not need to worry about an unplanned pregnancy, but it still comes with potential risks like STDs (sexually transmitted diseases) that can be transmitted orally. Some include Chlamydia, herpes, human papillomavirus (HPV), gonorrhea, syphilis, and HIV (human immunodeficiency virus). Save all sex for a monogamous marriage, use protection, and get tested! First Thessalonians 4:3-5 reminds us to abstain from sexual immorality so that we will know how to control our own body in sanctification and honor, not with lustful desires. Practice purity and holiness. It is worth it in the short term and long term.

- *No*, it is never okay for a man to lay his hands on you. Don't wait for it to get better or get worse; escape and get help. First John 4:18 reminds us that there is *no* fear in perfect love.

- *No*, you do not have to sleep with a man to earn his respect and trust. His proposal and a signed marriage certificate will do. We are allowing culture to teach us how to unwrap a gift from God; allow Christ to show you the value of purity. Save yourself from Sexually Transmitted Demons. True love is when you can get emotionally naked without being physically naked. Matthew 7:6 instructs us to not give what is holy to the dogs, nor cast our pearls to the swine. Know your worth, sis!

- No, it is not okay for a man to disrespect your name. Your family gave you that name; defend it proudly and with honor. Proverbs 22:1 reminds us that a good name is to be chosen rather than great riches.
- No, it is not okay for a man to manipulate your mind and have you thinking you are crazy for setting healthy boundaries. Believe the very first red flag. Run and don't look back! First Corinthians 13:4-6 reminds us what the opposite of love looks like: it does not envy or boast. It is not arrogant or rude. It does not insist on its own way. It is not irritable or resentful, and it does not rejoice in wrongdoing. Study what true love looks like so that you will pick up on the opposite without confusion or doubt.
- No, you cannot love someone into God's will. I have tried it, and it does not work. It will leave you sad, frustrated, and empty. You will become depleted in mind, body, and soul. You have to walk away, no matter how much it hurts. You have to let this person grow on their own terms. You can love and pray for that person from a distance, and you can give him or her to God. Only God can save and change hearts. Remember Jeremiah 29:12: *"Then you will call upon Me and go and pray to Me, and I will listen to you"* (NKJV).
- No, you are not crazy to want to be filled the same way you poured. This attitude of "What can you do for me?" will destroy any relationship, especially a marriage, because the other person will never perfectly meet your expectations. A selfish environment can easily produce feelings of bitterness, vengefulness, anger, and hostility. Choose relationships that are Christ focused, where one will try to outserve the other. Each will serve because it overflows from the Jesus in your hearts. Each will serve because you love. Each will serve because you've been loved. And, each will serve because you have been loved and served by the Father. John 15:10-11 (NIV), *"If you keep my commands, you will remain in my love, just as I have kept my Father's commands and remain in his love. 11 I have told you this so that my joy may be in you and that your joy may be complete."*
- No, it is not okay to abort the life growing inside of you just

because you feel bad for him, or it's bad timing. A true man will never set you up in this position in the first place, and will make sure you are secure with him in his plans to take care of his responsibility if a child is created. Choose the man you lay with wisely and choose a pregnancy option that does not add more trauma in your life. Children can add to your life in more ways than you can ever imagine. They bring "little gifts," the very thing you were missing in your life. Unplanned does not mean unwanted or unloved, yet it means that life knew what you needed before you even did. Sometimes what we see as an inconvenience for the moment can actually benefit you for a time to come! Psalm 126:3 says that children are a heritage from the Lord and the fruit of the womb is a reward.

- *No,* it is not okay to lower your standards for someone not trying to raise theirs. Do not conform to the standards of this world, but keep allowing God to transform you (Romans 12:2).
- *No,* you do not have to post your whole life on social media for views and likes. The only validation you need is from God. Do not set yourself up for a let-down trying to please people. And, if you do post, do not cause your "followers" to stumble and fall into sin. Uplift, encourage, and speak life into those who come across your page. Romans 14:13 reminds us to not to put any stumbling blocks or obstacles in our brother's or sister's way.
- *No,* you do not have to have all these material possessions to prove your worth to anyone. Find joy, peace, and satisfaction with the blessings God has given you in the present. We cannot take any of it with us when we die, so invest in the things that do matter. Matthew 6:20 reminds us to store up for ourselves treasures in heaven.
- *No,* not everyone is your friend and has your best interest at heart. Always take time to re-evaluate who is around you and for what purpose. Proverbs 18:24 (ESV) says, *"A man of many companions may come to ruin, but there is a friend who sticks closer than a brother."*
- And *no,* what you don't think you can find in a man does not

mean you will find it in a woman. God created us male and female with different roles that complement and empower each other, which is why the bond of marriage between a male and female is so powerful. It creates life physically, spiritually, and mentally that no other bond can create, which is why divorce is so detrimental individually and collectively to our society. Hebrews 13:4 says marriage is to be held in honor among all. Once you find your purpose, understand your value, and define your worth, woman of God, your walk, talk, and thought process will illuminate the presence of the Almighty God that will block out and scatter those devils, and attract those who truly are seeking the truth which you can share from your own testimony! Praise God!

ENTRY

This is a letter that I have written to my future husband, whoever God places into my life. It has been changed, revised, upgraded, and updated over the years because I have been. The more I grow in my faith and grow closer to the Lord, the more outdated this letter becomes. Every day is a new you. May your thoughts, desires, and wishes grow with you, especially when it comes to going into covenant with your future spouse.

Dear Future Husband:

I am waiting for you. I love you with all my heart. You are my Ephesians 5 man. My Joseph. A man who ran from temptation, blessed everything he touched, healed his heart during the time away from his family, and became a provider, protector, and blessing to his future generations. I want to grow with you. I want to spend the rest of my life with you. I want us to be best friends, lovers, encouragers, and cheerleaders for each other, and shoulders to cry on for one another. Let's talk. Let's communicate. I need you to speak life into my situations. Bring me back to the Word of God. Cover me with the Word of God. I need you to remind me of the goodness of God, the love of God. Speak my love language. May you be the Kingdom man that I need who looks in the mirror of Scripture. I pray that you value me because what a man values, he protects. I want us both to feel safe with each other and know that it is okay to be ourselves around each other. A safe place. I want to feel secure in that what I share with you, whether good or bad, will not be used against me to tear me down in those heated moments. I need you to pour into me and not let me run dry, and I do the same for you. I need you to let go of your past and never pick it back up. Lay it at the feet of Jesus.

I pray your heart has gone through heart rehabilitation because I need the entire healed you: one hundred percent. This covenant will never be fifty-fifty. Let's grow and build together. Let's be patient with each other in our seasons of "not yet." May you be able to speak to the queen in me and I be able to speak to the king in you. May neither one of us speak to and bring out the fool in each other. And most importantly, I need you to love Jesus more than you will ever love me. A man who loves Jesus will know how to love his wife. And I promise that God will be the number one man in my life as well. It is because of Him that I will know how to love you.

And Lord, help me to prepare for *You* before I prepare for my husband. My heart needs to be prepared for *You* first. Becoming one is hard, and I want to be on one accord with *You* first and foremost before this transition takes place. I do not want my relationship with You, Lord, or my future husband, to be a warzone. I put no confidence in this flesh. May I be holy, for You are holy, Lord. Thank You, Jesus, for this man You will bring into my life. Amen.

Here is space for my single sisters to begin your letter. I encourage that you write it in pencil so that changes can be made to yours as you grow, mature, and prosper in the Lord. Amen.

THE 4C HEART: Curls, Kinks, & Knots of My Dry, Thirsty, Single Soul

ENTRY

Lord, help me to be more feminine. Soften my thoughts, my words, my touch, and my desires. Help me to be more nurturing. Help me to be more helpful, more caring, and kind. Soften my demeanor. Help me to smile more. Help me to be a woman. I have lost my way. I have had to be two people in one for so long when raising my children that I have forgotten how to be me, a woman. I have had to take on the masculine role for so long that I have forgotten how to be me, a woman. I have had to be so tough, rough, and hard due to life circumstances that I have forgotten to be me, a woman. Fill me with the delicacies of womanhood that I may pour out a different strength. A strength that only women possess. The strength that comes from being so close to the heartbeat of Christ. Lord, help me to be so close to You that it pulsates through my very being in everything that I touch, say, and do so that I can grow to be me, a woman. Amen.

ENTRY

Lord, my heart is so heavy. You have brought to my attention of the importance of *covenants*. A covenant is an agreement, a contract, a pledge, a commitment. And, God, you are *covenant keeping*. The promise you gave us. You are in control, and what You started, You will finish. But, God, everything You do, Satan imitates, and some of us have made covenants with him. Some of us have made blood covenants with the devil through abortions, premarital sex, divorce, drugs and alcohol, adultery, homosexuality, witchcraft, voodoo, ancestral worship, horoscope and palm readings, sage burning, crystal energy and chakras, yoga and meditation, sorority pledges, Eastern Star and Masonic affiliations, unforgiveness, revenge, rebellion against / disrespecting our parents . . . etc. The worst part is that some of us do not even the know the covenant(s) we have made with the devil, and it continues in our bloodlines to the next generation. This is why they are so hard to break and change from. This is why we have generational curses! Just like God has a plan for our lives, to set us free, the devil has a plan for our life, to keep us in bondage.

Woman of God, it is time to put an end to this! The enemy is in *high treason* against the Most High! A restraining order has been placed on him when Jesus died on the cross. The same spirit that raised Jesus from the dead, we have in us! It is time to rise up, woman of God! There is nothing more mighty than a woman of God who understands *covenant*. It is time to break that addiction, break that family history of cancer and disease, break that demonic possession, break that cycle of abuse, break that lustful spirit, break the gluttony spirit, break that witchcraft spirit, break that Jezebel spirit, in Jesus' name!

Walk in the power and anointing of the Holy Spirit. Remove those mountains! Rebuke the devil and he will flee! This is what we carry! We carry the power to break yokes; to rebuke unholy blood covenants; to pray in the spirit over our family, children, and generations; to shape and mold the future; to restore and take back what the enemy has tried to take away. Know who you are, woman of God. Know your worth. Know your value. And most importantly, understand covenant.

"*My people are destroyed from lack of knowledge . . .* " (Hosea 4:6 NIV).

May this be you and your family no more! Amen.

ENTRY

When Eve in the Bible sinned, she changed the future and future generations. When you sin, you change the future for your future generations. This is deep. Woman of God, what you carry is so important. How you move, how and what you speak, how you conduct yourself, how you pray, how you seek God's face, how you manage your house and home, how you love your family members, how you support your husband, how you raise your children . . . etc. will shape and mold the future. We must grow in love, laugh with joy, keep the peace, cultivate patience, speak with kindness, embrace goodness, commit to faithfulness, and develop self-control. Ezekiel 18:31-32 (NKJV) says,

> *Cast away from you all the transgressions which you have committed, and get yourselves a new heart and a new spirit. For why should you die, O house of Israel? For I have no pleasure in the death of one who dies,"* says the Lord God. *"Therefore turn and live!"*

Women of God, we are the life-givers on this earth. God gave only us this special gift and responsibility. Let's not continue this cycle of sin and keep creating the generation of *Cain* who will continue to spill innocent blood. Let's break the cycle and create a generation of *Abels* who will hear the voice of God, will walk in obedience, and will stand in righteousness as they will do things God's way. Let's plead the blood of Christ Jesus over this future generation. Let's *turn* and *live*. Amen.

ENTRY

Talking with a friend today and listening to her cry about her situation. It breaks my heart that we as women are constantly comparing ourselves to what other women are doing and achieving in their season. Or, the amount of pressure we put on ourselves trying to achieve multiple titles, positions . . . etc. Or what society is telling us we should be doing and achieving by this age or that age.

By whose standard? Who told you that? Whatever we allow in our ear impacts our sight. Quit listening to what "everybody" is saying and focus on what God is telling you. When we shut those voices up, we can start to hear Him more clearly. Some of us think God is silent because He is not speaking what we prefer. But it is not about us.

Let's get our preferences and priorities straight. Let's get rid of this worldly vision and start looking through *Kingdom* lenses. Let's get our hearts transformed and our minds renewed. When we do those things, we will start to see that God is working something new in us in our season of "not yet." We will learn that He is the author of this thing called life, not us. We have done enough messing up, don't you think?

As women, we will need to learn what a lot of us have such a hard time doing, and that is that uncomfortable little s-word: submit! This takes an unbelievable amount of strength. Submission takes place when we learn how to listen and do things God's way. When our will is broken and molded to God's will. Keeping a correct perspective of God's love and way for our lives is the greatest source of empowerment for women.

We have got to quit listening to the lie that we need to be all things to everybody (this scripture has been completely taken out of context to justify living a compromising lifestyle). *No!*

We need to be everything to God so that He can use us to represent Him to all people. This is what it means to be Christlike. In this place of submission is where we reach our potential and find our purpose. We will not need to chase what the world says we should achieve and have by this time and age only for it to change in the next couple of years. The world does not have the answers; it only repeats and regurgitates.

But in God is wisdom and newness. His Word never changes and yet lives on. Find rest and peace in that. Find joy and freedom in that! Our heavenly Father wants to empower, protect, honor, confide in, and celebrate you in every way, every day. He has set the standard. Reach for it. Fully discover who you are in Him.

My sister, embrace who you are in Him and allow your dry, thirsty soul to be drenched, encouraged, empowered, and strengthened. Amen.

> "but they who wait for the LORD shall renew their strength; they shall mount up with wings like eagles; they shall run and not be weary; they shall walk and not faint" (Isaiah 40:3).

Closing Thought and Prayer

The trick of the enemy is to attack your identity in Christ Jesus. This is done by planting seeds of doubt in our minds. We need to understand our identities, women of God. We need to know our identity is secure in Jesus and that we have *nothing* to prove.

We have the perfect example laid out for us in Word of God in Matthew 4:1-7. In this passage, we see the devil trying to trip up Jesus and cause Him to stumble and doubt himself. Both Jesus and the devil knew the Scripture and used the Scripture. (If the devil knows the scriptures, ladies, you better know it for yourself!) Hide it in your hearts so that you do not sin against God (Psalms 119:11).

In Matthew 4:6, we see that the devil chose his words perfectly in his questioning to Jesus:

> and said to Him, "If You are the Son of God, throw Yourself down. For it is written: 'He shall give His angels charge over you,' and, 'In their hands they shall bear you up, Lest you dash your foot against a stone.'" (NKJV).

See that key word "*if*"? Satan already knew who Jesus was. He did not need to question that. But his question was to appeal to the pride of life. So many times we find ourselves in situations trying to prove ourselves to others because they questioned our identity. Now, as a result, we are out here looking crazy. Now, we did or said something that we cannot take back. And, for what? That person who challenged you is long gone, has served their purpose, and you are left to pick up the broken pieces. It is like we have this intrinsic need to have approval stamped by others to prove who we are. Is this necessary? What "*if*" seeds have we allowed others to plant into our lives? How much pride have we allowed unchecked in our hearts and has, in turn, shifted our desires, focus, and direction?

The temptation in this scenario was not about questioning His name, but the motivation of Jesus' heart. Your heart. Are the desires of your heart lined up with God's desires or your own? Which desires take up the *ultimate* residence in your life? Are you secure in Jesus enough to have the response that He had in verse 7? *"Jesus said to him, "It is written again, 'You shall not tempt the Lord your God.'"* (NKJV). Boom, Satan! Your God has spoken.

Yes, the devil was created just like the rest of us. Jesus knew who he was. There was no "*if*"s about it. The rest of what the devil said was irrelevant. Jesus did not have to prove Himself by doing anything but by *being* who He was. We need to be the same way, women of God.

We will not need to prove ourselves to anyone if we know our identity in Christ Jesus. You are *God's child*. Speak it, believe it, and be it! Know who you are! And, know that we cannot overcome temptation without complete dependence on God. We cannot overcome temptation when we let our pride overtake us and we feel the need to prove ourselves to others for their praise and attention. No! Our worth comes from God alone. Our identity comes from God alone. Stay in His presence. Stay in His favor. Line your desires up with His. Find your purpose and calling in Him. Allow Him to move in your life. So when that pride of life tries to raise its ugly head and question your identity and bring doubt, you can tell that old devil what the Bible say about being a woman of God:

Luke 1:45 (NKJV): *"Blessed is she who believed, for there will be a fulfillment of those things which were told her from the Lord."*

Proverbs 31:25 (NKJV): *"Strength and honor are her clothing; She shall rejoice in time to come."*

Proverbs 3:15 (NKJV): *"She is more precious than rubies, And all the things you may desire cannot compare with her."*

Psalms 46:5 (NKJV): *"God is in the midst of her, she shall not be moved; God shall help her, just at the break of dawn."*

Lord, help us to find ourselves in You. Help us to find our purpose and calling in You. Heal us from the wounds and hurts of our past and present. Help us to be whole in You. May our desires line up with Your desires. Help us to be holy, for You are holy. Soften our hearts to be malleable to Your ways and Your will. May we have a hunger and thirst for righteousness. May we hide Your Word in our hearts that we may not sin against You.

Lord, please uproot the seeds of doubt, fear, lust, and pride that were planted into our lives. Fill us with Your perfect love, wisdom, knowledge, understanding, peace, and joy. Touch our hearts, minds, bodies, and souls with Your precious healing balm. Quench our dry, thirsty hearts with waters that never run dry. And may we walk toward newness in You that only You can provide when we are fully dependent on You. Thank You for hearing our heart cries. Thank You for helping us embrace our womanhood. We love You, Lord. In Jesus' name. Amen.

Now go! Much work is to be done!

My dear SISTER:

Strong
Inspirator
So
That
Everyone around her
Reflects her beauty

(1 Timothy 2:9-10; 1 Peter 3:3-4)

"The Lord bless you and keep you;
The Lord make His face shine upon you,
And be gracious to you;
The Lord lift up His countenance upon you,
And give you peace" (Numbers 6:24-26 NKJV).

The Lord loves you and knows you by name. When He formed you in the womb, you were fearfully and wonderfully made (Psalms 139:13-14). He has called for you, and you have a purpose. Answer the call! Do not fear or doubt. You have been fully equipped and have been given a sound mind (2 Timothy 1:7). He has blessed you to be a blessing to others. The Lord is by your side. Walk in your anointing and victory! Amen.

Always,
Your SISTER, Anna~

"Blessed is she who believed, for there will be a fulfillment of those things which were told her from the Lord" Luke 1:45 (NKJV).

About the Author

Anna currently resides in North Carolina and has two children, Jayden and Janiah. Her passion is speaking with women and helping them through their difficult situations in life, especially when it comes to an unplanned pregnancy. From someone who has personally gone through abortions, miscarriages, separation and divorce, anxiety, depression, emotional and sexual abuse, and single parenting pains, writing has been a way for her to process through her thoughts. She has decided to gather and share her life experiences, her cries, and her prayers with you in hopes that you can be encouraged, especially if you can relate. She understands what it is to be a woman, the journey of womanhood, and the importance of sharing her life journey with others—just for other women to hear that they are not the only ones in the world going through their situations makes all the difference in the world. It gives hope in what one may have thought was a hopeless situation.

My dear sisters, may this series bless your dry, thirsty souls, and bring healing to your land. In Jesus' name. Amen.

4cheartseries@gmail.com

Read More

I hope that my book series helps and encourages you in your emotional and spiritual walk throughout this thing called life. May you be blessed and healed in Jesus' name. Amen.

Book 1: Words for Seasons: Journal Entries of My Life Story
Link: amzn.to/3c8bUq9

www.ingramcontent.com/pod-product-compliance
Lightning Source LLC
Chambersburg PA
CBHW072105110526
44590CB00018B/3323